MEDITATIONS ON JUDAISMS AND THE PECULIAR CASE OF YESHU

YISHMAEL ben ABUYA

MEDITATIONS ON JUDAISMS AND THE PECULIAR CASE OF YESHU

iUniverse books may be ordered through booksellers or by contacting:

iUniverse
1663 Liberty Drive
Bloomington, IN 47403
www.iuniverse.com
1-800-Authors (1-800-288-4677)

Because of the dynamic nature of the Internet, any web addresses or links contained in this book may have changed since publication and may no longer be valid. The views expressed in this work are solely those of the author and do not necessarily reflect the views of the publisher, and the publisher hereby disclaims any responsibility for them.

Any people depicted in stock imagery provided by Thinkstock are models, and such images are being used for illustrative purposes only. Certain stock imagery © Thinkstock.

ISBN: 978-1-5320-3923-2 (sc)
ISBN: 978-1-5320-3924-9 (e)

Library of Congress Control Number: 2018901323

Print information available on the last page.

iUniverse rev. date: 01/26/2018

DEDICATION

I dedicate this book to and for

THE SIX MILLIOM

ELIMITED DURING THE TIME OF THE HOLOCAUST

{roughly the time of Hitler's, reign}

LOSS

Such is the opening of this book. The word came to me as the lyrics of "MacCather Park" wafted through the open window. I dare not cite the lyrics. If I cited them verbatim I would be sued. {Or maybe no-one would care anyway.} The poison of Loss and Fear surrounds me as I cite my favorite lyric and as I cite this great production, "McCather Park." Enough!

"I'll never have that recipe again; OHHH NOOOOOO!!!"

*****   *****   *****

PROLOG

{by way of opening [there is] *the creating of God along with the Heavens and the Earth"}*

Those are weighty questions, Duane; and they are not just theoretical. I can tell by the way you express them. For answers to those kinds of questions I usually charge a hundred and fifty per hour. For you I'll give you the discount. Just send me seventy-five./// To be straight forward, the "beyond" world simply does not exist. What is Holy is shot through with what we jerkily call the "phenomenal" world. Except for the Goddess of Truth — who honors the so-called 'phenomenal' — the Tradition of the so-called "philosophers" tends, at best, to give it a secondary status or, at worst, just plain trashes it. The reality is that the noumenal obtains AS the phenomenal. Plato came to see all of this in his last two decades of writing. But — paradoxically — more than anyone else he was responsible for that "beyond"-oriented world-view he invented for the first two decades of his serious philosophy. Christianity almost wholesale (along with Islam) has bought into that META-physical schema. Most versions of Judaism do as well <including, most especially, <including, most

especially, Qabbalah>. But there are very significant strains which do not.///

The world really is full of Gods. That is not necessarily comforting, but it is true. Mystery does not belong with the so-called "beyond" for the simple reason that there is no "beyond." The Holy (which includes the daimonic) is all around of us all of the time. So too with mystery. Mystery is, for the most part, not comforting. There are diabolical dimensions to it. It is more dark than light. Divinity/God is not incomprehensible. We are in it and it is dark. Comprehensible but not comforting; troubling; even dreadful. But evident only for those who do not live in DENIAL.

I have maintained that only such an overall concatenation of such things is the case. And, in the final analysis, I aver, it is better that "there be" life than not. Such is my EMUNAH (some say AMUNAH). MY TRUST. I would say that if you look for the Holy and God in the so-called "beyond" you will never find it.

***** ***** ***** ***** *****

EVEN A BROKEN VASE MAY HAVE BEAUTY

Think of me carrying a large purple Vase and I trip bringing the vase into large, medium, small, and miniscule pieces. Once the vase was whole. No longer. Now the beautiful vase — the large pieces; the median pieces; the small pieces; and the miniscule pieces. It's akin in some way to Humpty Dumpty who fell off a wall and could never be brought to the way he was. Once a beautiful vase now swept up the pieces and shards for the garbage. Some, of course, were miniscule dust entities which ended up "blowing in the wind." Larger pieces and even smaller pieces were saved by the owner and brought them back to his room.

These pieces of the vase represent what happened to my proposed book. A broken vase; a broken book. The owner could not bear to lose all of what he owned; indeed (and curiously) he brought most of both the large and small pieces of the vase back to his room. He liked what he kept. You might like it too.

Come and meditate with me.

*****   *****   *****   *****   *****
*****   *****   *****
*****   *****   *****   *****   *****

THERE IS THIS AS WELL:

There are a number of somewhat diverse figures in this endeavor. But far and away the focus is on Yeshu: his endemic Jewishness; his blasphemy; and his deep humanism especially after the *imbroglio* dealing with the farce 'Resurrection' of Lazarus.' I limit my accountings to all the figures of the book insofar they are accounted as HUMANS and ONLY HUMANS <even if anyone of them or others claim to be more than HUMANS or even claim divinity>. No more, no less. To be sure such an accounting of the main figures — including Yeshu — are of fallibility. I certainly "wash my hands" <so to speak> *vis-à-vis* of any claims of divinity.

A perfect Human is, simply, not a Human; it's that simple.

*****

Finally, you will note that just below the title of the title page there is a small parenthetical phrase:

{a novel}

In the final analysis I am a novelist. Yes, there is much in the book which is not usually called "a novel." Yes, the book is filled with factual matters. Even so, I put forth accountings based on the major figures in this "novel." A novelist attempts to go into the brains and emotions of the characters. But no-one will know for sure whether or not what is in the brains and emotions of these characters. Indeed, what is in the brains and emotions of the characters <including me> are not always congruent with what comes out their speech and their emotions. Take it or Leave it. It's just a novel.

CONTENTS

MEDITATION ONE

We begin with The TORAH. 'TORAH' has several meanings. 'TORAH' is the Way.' More to our situation "Torah" is the name of the Jewish Bible and Sacred Scripture, known as the TANACH <which is an acronym for the three portions of Scripture: 'TORAH'; Nevi'm; and Qethuvim>. These three over a long time came to gel as what came to be called "THE TANAKH" which constitutes Jewish Scripture: The Tanakh

Scripture, then is divided into three sections: THE TORAH; Nevi'im; and QET(h)UVIM. TORAH and Nevi'im <The Prophets>; are considered as REVELATION with the caveat that the degree of REVELATION of the book TORAH is considered to hold the most Revelation for those who can deal with it. The book NEVI'IM, it is considered, that its offerings bring a lesser degree of REVELATION <albeit, dealing with Nevi'im is NOT a holiday; they are tough>. QETUVIM offers a great deal of wisdom <albeit it, in the technical sense, it is not considered as bringing forth REVELATION>.

1

<<<<<As I recall, QET(h)UVIM was put together at the Yavne Community (opened circa 70 ad and beyond). Likewise this was the time when Rabbi Aqiba set in motion the MISHNA which would be a compilation of the Pharisaic *halakhot* which had grown exponentially like weeds. It was always understood that the Oral Torah ***would NEVER, NEVER, NEVER, <u>EVER</u>***, be subjected to a WRITTEN compilation. Some things are sacred and, indeed, "Some" can handle, rightly, "The Sacred"; others claim "the sacred" but fall short of truly engaging "the sacred." Think of Rabbi Aqiba. He took it upon himself to do what was forbidden: a WRTTEN!!!!! compilation of the <putative> ORAL Torah. Some things are sacred and, indeed, "<u>Some</u>" can handle, rightly, "the sacred"; others claim "the sacred" but fall short of truly engaging "the sacred." Think of Rabbi Aqiba. He took it upon <u>just by himself</u> to do what was forbidden: he put forth the Halakha **<u>in writing!</u>** SHAME!.>>>>>

To be fair, the proliferation of *halakhot* did balloon to ridiculous ranges. Rabbi Aqiba took it upon himself to put forth the huge (and ever ballooning) of *halakhot* <u>IN WRITING!</u> The ever-growing amount of *halakhot* was huge and still proliferating <like weeds>. So everybody "winked" and allowed that the *halakhot* would be allowed to put to writing. But proliferation never stopped.

In any case, Yeshu was very clear in distinguishing several matters. To wit:

Those ten *MITSVOT* from Scripture in stone on tablets at Sinai which belongs now in "THE TORAH" without tablets. At some point over the centuries involved, the original and actual tablets seem to have disappeared over those centuries one way or another.

*****

The putative ORAL TORAH *halakhot* claimed by the Pharisees is somewhat tangled. The Pharisaic Sect —((that is when they will have come into being since the earliest proto-Pharisees didn't arrive on the scene until the early fifth century *bc* meaning that there were a number of centuries EARLIER dealing with the early tablets at Sinai along with writers who wrote what would come to be Scripture.)) Back then no-one even brought up anything like a putative "Oral Torah." Rather, there were Scripters building what would be, eventually, the Jewish TORAH over a period of centuries.

Oral Torah was born — IN FACT — at the time (early fifth century) when the Pharisees allegedly first came on the scene!!!). The Pharisees fixated on the claim that the ORAL TORAH was generated at the same time when those tablets were generated at Sinai. Not even Possible.

Of the true earliest groupings the *Soferim* stands out. It was a Scripturally based < albeit it would be a long time before Scripture was closed>. The *Soferim* <later they used the heading "Scribes"> came into being *circa* from the seventh century bce turning into the fifth century bce. And they, most certainly (since they were Scripturally oriented <such as Scripture was at that time>), were NOT interested, later, as the Proto-Pharisees morphed into the waning sixth century *bce* turning into the fifth century *bce*.

The reality seems to point to this: The only Sect which is known back then to have something-like an Oral Torah "claim" was the that of the proto-Pharisees. It would not take a "Sherlock Holmes" to figure out that there was, in fact, NO generation of the Oral Torah until the Proto-Pharisees invented the putative "Oral Torah" circa early fifth century *bce*.

At the **very earliest**, something like a community already fixated on a putative Oral Torah appears to have emerged. Yes, as we have seen above, what would come, eventually, to be the "Pharisaic" Sect emerged as the sixth century *bce* was becoming the early fifth century, bce. This group came to be the major Sect in Judaism; indeed on into to our own time for better or for worse. But one thing is for sure. This Sect which promotes the Oral Torah to such a way that, in various ways, it impinges deleteriously upon the Scripture-centric 'denominations' which is not healthy for Judaism. The Pharisaic grouping then and now — insofar as they *de facto* <<<but they would never admit to such>>> — honor their precious Oral Torah over Scripture. And that is wrong.

> {{Was there in fact that there were Oral Torah *halakhot* which somehow passed down a Huge set of *halakhot* from Sinai over a period of almost two millennia? And, putatively, all of this happened before there was a Pharisaic Sect which would claim that they were the Sect which was the recipient of all those putative *halakhot*. (Nice, if you can sell it; apparently it worked for them.) The reality was that the Proto Pharisees invented the the "Oral Torah" as the

> sixth century became the fifth century ce
> and continuing not only into the fourth
> century but continuing up to our time.}}

All in all, I suggest, that **only** the tablets were given to the Jews <u>at that time at Sinai</u>. And that was enough at that time. There were simply the ten commandments from the *Mitsvot* on those tablets regardless of the putative Oral Torah **CLAIMS** at Sinai. Indeed, in effect, there was a HUGE discrepancy between the Pharisees on the one hand with their putative Oral Torah whereas the others were satisfied with the Scriptural account at Sinai which does not include Oral Torah benefits. Of course, the Pharisees also studied the WRITTEN revelation at Sinai — along with the putative <u>ORAL</u> TORAH which ended up with the **ORAL** revelation in writing anyway. Thanks to Rabbi Aqiba <for better or for worse>.

*****　*****　*****　*****　*****
*****　*****　*****
*****　*****　*****　*****　*****

Keep this in mind as well. It is found in *Matthew* 23:1-3. One must be careful when we cite anything in the New Testament with regard to Yeshu since **SO MUCH** of such is **<u>NOT</u>** — for various reasons which will be explored — rooted in that person called "Yeshu."

Nonetheless, Matthew 23:1-3 seems valid. Listen:

"Then addressing the people and the diciples, Yeshu said: **The Scribes and the Pharisees occupy the CHAIR OF MOISHE.** *You must, accordingly, do what they tell you and listen to what they say.* But do not be guided by what they actually DO.

*****   *****   *****   *****   *****

*****   *****   *****

*****   *****   *****   *****   *****

In any case it is clear that there was a growing tension between Yeshu and the Pharisees. As time went on, Yeshu became more and more "slicing" in his encounters with the Pharisees. In turn the Pharisees drummed out for all to hear that Yeshu was a *mamzer*.

*****

Again, it is quintessentially Jewish, then as well as now, to argue over the *Halakha*. But both of the parties <the Pharisees and Yeshu> to the dispute maintain clear and unambiguous dietary mandates. The two parties are infinitely closer to each other than a position <<articulated in *MARK* 7:19>> which allegedly eschews the heart and soul of Judaism as false and concocted. More than that, **a Yeshu which, allegedly, eschews the heart and soul of Judaism is a false and concocted "Yeshu." Yet that is exactly for those who never saw Yeshu in the flesh. The so-called "Fathers of the Church" created a Yeshu largely lacking the only thing which animated Yeshu in the flesh: <u>HIS JEWISHNESS TO HIS VERY BONES.</u>** Christianity ended up running on a concocted vision of Yeshu; a Yeshu which, <u>at most</u>, has a **veneer** of Jewishness. In other words this gigantic religion centers itself on veneer; no substance.

*****

Turning now to *Matthew* 23:1-3. <<Yeshu speaking; *encore*>>:

Then, <again>, addressing the people and his disciples, Yeshu said: *The* Scribes *and the Pharisees occupy the CHAIR OF MOISHE. You must, accordingly, do what they tell you and listen to what they say.* But do not be guided by what they actually DO since they do not practice what they preach.

8

[Matthew 23:1-3]

Stern, but not outrageous — *since they do not practice what they preach.*

My! My! **IF** these words <i.e., *they do not practice what they preach*> are from Yeshu chances are that he is "low-balling" the imperfection. After all, who can say that they always {{{yes, even ***Yeshu***}}} practice what they teach? Yeshu was often calm and serene as he is in this case.

But Yeshu could be ***mercurial to a fault***

*****

In any case, everything changes starting with verse four and continuing on to the end of the Chapter. However, before we address that — indeed— excoriating passage from four to the end of the Chapter, let us pause on this opening offering from Chapter Twenty-Three. Yeshu who has a real beef with the Pharisees (and vice versa) — also recognizes here, "the Scribes" as well as the Pharisees. After all they are, in theory, Scripture-centric as was Yeshu. Way back they were referred as *Soferim* ((this grouping is reviewed in detail in another section of this production; the *Soferim*)).

Eventually the *Soferim* morphed into "The Scribes." They were still Scripture-oriented.

*****   *****   *****

> *Halakha* functions as the whole recipient of the many *halakhot* (in plural). Along with the uppercase "H" the word is simply all the whole of the *halakhot*. Both terms <'Halakha' and *halakhot*> emerge from the Pharisees. There are, of course, the *Mitsvot* of Scripture and they are NOT *halakhot* even though the Halakha Itself includes not only the *halakhot* but the *Mitsvot* of Scripture as well; it is just idiocentric.

*****   *****   *****

Continuing on.

More than that, **a putative Yeshu which, allegedly, eschews the heart and soul of Judaism would be a false and concocted "Yeshu."** It's not whether or not one has seen Yeshu and bandied with Yeshu in the flesh **OR NOT**. Over the centuries from when Yeshu roamed Israel/Palestine right up to the present day there is but one coin which opens up a relationship with Yeshu. To wit:

HIS OR HER <u>JEWISHNESS TO ONE'S VERY MARROW OF ONE'S BONES</u>

Yes that is exactly what, usually, those who never saw Yeshu in the flesh, can rely and have relied upon on that beautiful caveat:

HIS OR HER <u>JEWISHNESS TO ONE'S VERY MARROW OF ONE'S BONES</u>

```
*****   *****   *****   *****   *****
*****   *****   *****
*****   *****   *****   *****   *****
```

In radical contrast those "Fathers of the Church" attempted to ignore the Jewishness of Yeshu. Yes: even if Yeshu were pushed to a corner [albeit Yeshu was long buried] they would have to acknowledge that the Jewish rock-solid status of Yeshu as a Jew is simply the case. But those "Fathers of the Church" [[[— this would be going on through the second part of the first century *ad* and onward through the third century ad and beyond —]]] hemmed and hawed trying to pretend that, somehow, Yeshu "really" was not Jewish. After a while it came to be the case that Christians "allowed"

11

that Yeshu was *really, really, really,* Jewish. But the deepest knot was shared with Jews one way <i.e., following the *Halakha*> and Christians another way. The Christians radically eschewed the *Halakha* in favor for a dietary menu which would be best as *Halakha*-lite; **very lite**. Yeshu would laugh and cry about this "down-loading" of just who he was. A JEW. Period.

What about God?

For the Jews it was simple: There is ONLY ONE GOD and it ain't Yeshu. Furthermore, Yeshu had an idiosyncratic claim which knocks out the possibility of a plain simple ONE GOD anyway. The God (s) that Yeshu was claiming was an idiosyncratic accounting of a putative God which might be called 'two-fold'. I am referring to the claim of Yeshu to the effect that — and famously —:

THE FATHER AND I ARE ONE

Of course that would be a Blasphemy from the position of Judaism. It is the stain on Yeshu insofar as his treasured Blasphemy albeit that that noun, "Blasphemy", was not the meaning **for Yeshu** as he experienced the "blasphemy." He took comfort in this blasphemy. <<Indeed early in his ministry

he somehow suppressed what he was claiming>>. Even so, blasphemy is blasphemy. He had set in motion an accounting of a putative God which can be called 'two-fold.'

Shame on Yeshu. It effected his standing as a Jew. Compromised enough that his endemic Judaism will always carry that stain. That said, the heavenly Court would simply put an asterick by his name in the Heavenly register <so to speak>. No doubt, this was a man who did go astray on a very important matter. Even so, Yeshu was born a Jew; he was circumcised; lived as a Jew <even with that "asterick">; and died as a Jew. In a word, HE WAS JEWSISH IN THE MARROW OF HIS BONES.

*****

Yes, Yes, Yes. I hear you. This claim of Yeshu points to what later — for Christians — would call a "Trinity"; a putative "Holy Trinity": The Father; The Son; and the Holy Spirit. From a Jewish perspective it doesn't matter that Yeshu's God had two dimensions and later, Christianity, three dimensions. In both cases there is blasphemy.

YISHMAEL ben ABUYA

The bottom line goes back to Judaism:

There is ONLY **ONE** GOD

No duality; no trinity

<u>JUST THE ONE AND ONLY GOD</u>

***** ***** ***** ***** *****
***** ***** *****
***** ***** ***** ***** *****

TIME-OUT:

True Jews don't need to be coaxed into WHAT THEY <u>ALREADY HAVE</u>. There were almost FOUR MILLENNIA of Judaism before it happened that an Israeli father soldier <who had been conscripted into the Roman Army as an Archer> bivouacked into the somewhat shabby shack of a youngish maiden who lived alone. The outcome was that she became quickly pregnant by that Archer. She never saw the Archer again. He was the father of Yeshu. His name was Pantera. <more to come>.

TIME-OUT OVER

*****

Christianity ended up running on a concocted vision of Yeshu; a putative Yeshu which, <u>at most</u>, was but a **veneer** of Jewishness. In other words this gigantic religion <i.e., Christianity> centers itself on veneer; no substance. The Christian "Yeshu" <aka "Jesus"> never existed.

*****

This matter is difficult. Those who never saw Yeshu is gigantic. Saul/Paul is one of them. I am one of them. My own assessment is that Saul/Paul never really connected to Yeshu FOR A VERY GOOD REASON: YESHU WAS ALREADY DEAD. Saul/Paul was taking too much time in those letters wherein Paul used Yeshu as a mirror which would glorify Paul himself.

In any case writing about Yeshu requires to go deep into one's own soul and own both the good and the atrocious in one's being. In any case, I see no evidence that Saul/Paul ever went to his own soul and own both the good and the atrocious in one's very being. And if you maintain you or anyone maintains that he or she never embided the atrocious is only skimming in one's life.

*****

ENCORE:

Then, addressing the people and his disciples, Yeshu said: "The Scribes and the Pharisees occupy the CHAIR OF MOISHE. You must, accordingly, do what they tell you and listen to what they say. But do not be guided by what they actually DO since they do not practice what they preach.

[Matthew 23:1-3]

My! My! **IF** these words <i.e., *they do not practice what they preach*> are from Yeshu, chances are that he is "low-balling" the imperfection. After all, who can say that they always {{{yes, even Yeshu}}} practice what they teach. Yeshu was often calm and serene as he is in this case. But Yeshu could also be ***mercurial to a fault***.

In any case, everything changes starting with verse four and continuing to the end of the Chapter. However, before we address that excoriating passage from verse four to the end of the Chapter, let us pause on this opening from Chapter Twenty-Three. Yeshu — who has a real beef with the Pharisees (and *vice versa*) — also recognizes here "the Scribes" as well as the Pharisees. After all they, the Scribes, are, in theory, Scripture-centric <i.e., Jewish Scripture> as was Yeshu. Way back then they were referred to as *Soferim* ((this grouping is reviewed in detail in another section of this production)).

MEDITATION TWO

Some have maintained <wisely> that the 'ur'-
Fourth Gospel with its Hellenic aura was written
by one who perhaps Yeshu knew more than anyone
else. I am speaking of the young man, Lazarus.
(i.e., *"Elazar"* and, and for some, *"Eliezer"* in
Hebrew).

Stripped of the Hellenic overlay of this Gospel
— an overlay brought TO this ur-text — <i.e.,
what would expand to become the part of the
fourth Gospel almost a century after this "ur-
Gospel" was written by Lazarus,> This Gospel is,
paradoxically, the most Semitic of all the Gospels.
Lazarus put it on the shelf, so to speak, until he
was near death.

Lazarus came from a wealthy family <all Jewish>
and influential in Bethany. Lazarus was well
known by high Roman officials as well as High
Jewish officials. By virtue of his family's wealth
and status doors were opened to Lazarus ((and
continued thereof)) which most of the followers
of Yeshu could not even aspire to such. It was
through this avenue — "The Bethany Road"

19

— that the lowly (but tall) Nazarean — came to be received in "higher society."

The Greek/Hellenic overlay of this fourth Gospel occurred almost a century posterior to the original manuscript produced by Lazarus (*aka* "Elazar"; *aka* Eliezer) back in the day <i.e., soon after Yeshu died>. As we shall see below, "Lazarus," back then, put the document under wraps and turned back to a fuller Jewish-centric life. Towards the very end of his life he allowed the manuscript to be disseminated to a few Jews who had heard about the document. The emergent "Fathers of the Church" would have had to do something so as to temp down the piece of dynamite which "Lazarus" (now very old and near death) put forth. When "Lazarus" was on his death bed he put his own manuscript in the hands of his son who, eventually, sold it to a collector who in turn brought this piece of dynamite to a Jewish merchant. The Jewish merchant read the entire manuscript and realized it was something which must be disseminated.

It was not long after that Jewish merchant's dissemination of the manuscript that the "Fathers of the Church" got a copy of this incredible manuscript. Yes again: it was dynamite. It was too late to sink totally. Those Fathers decided, accordingly, to intrude into the manuscript an overlay of Hellenic intrusions into the manuscript. However, worse than that, there were some deletions as those Fathers realized JUST HOW **JEWISH** was this manuscript. The Fathers, then, did what they could do to "soften" the clearly Jewish manuscript. The result was a ridiculous mélange.

Even so, Jewish readers immediately had the ability to ignore the Hellenic features forced upon the manuscript; they were pretty obvious. Even with this gross intrusion the portions of the Lazarus' manuscript was still fairly intact after all those years.

*****   *****   *****   *****   *****

*****   *****   *****

*****   *****   *****   ******   *****

Listen now to this accounting of the one who was referred to as "the other disciple" <who hailed from a rich family in Bethany in contrast to the regular followers of Yeshu most of whom were paupers>. Lazarus was not one of the now-and-then "twelve," most of whom were poor: "rag-tag" followers, many from the Galilee. In any case, note Lazarus' intimacy with money and "Big Shots" was greater than any of the others, including Shimon Peter.

By the way; on that Thursday night, Shimon-Peter came to be locked out of the meeting room wherein would finalize Yeshu's outcome. Listen:

Shimon-Peter (aka, "The Rock")*, *with another disciple* [i.e., that other disciple <Lazarus>] *followed Yeshu. This "other" disciple — who was known by the High Priest— with Yeshu went into the High Priest's palace* <<i.e., the scene of Caiaphas' huge dining room>>. *But the guard did not recognize* Shimon Peter *and did not allow to Shimon Peter. So the "other disciple," the one known by the High Priest, went out and spoke to the woman who was keeping the door and allowed "The Rock" to enter.*

[John 18: 15—17]

> *.[[There were two "Shimons." The famous one was "Shimon"/"Peter." The other "Shimon" was the one who accompanied Judas (the treasurer) that night to get up to Nazareth as quickly as possible so that James/Jacob could cool down Yeshu who was who was acting strange <even for Yeshu>. But it was too late.]]

Just for the record, the "other disciple" <and sometimes "the beloved disciple"> was Lazarus.

I will stop there, for now. I just wanted for the context of this section of my production to offer, for overall context, a sense of "the other disciple" and how bonded he was to Yeshu <and the big shots.>. The forthcoming passage also testifies to the status of the family of that "other disciple" from Bethany.

[This "other" disciple ended up having an amazing Jewish "career" **long after** Yeshu was buried. He was a major player in the foundation of the Yavne Community (70ad) and, as well, a major player for the first two decades or so of that Yavne Community.]

Lazarus: Elazar; Eliezer. In English it comes our "Lazarus." In Hebrew there are two spellings for one person: "Elazar" or "Eliezer." By the way, "EL" is one of the names of God in Hebrew.

Without doubt whatsoever, this Lazarus was the "Beloved Apostle" and, virtually, just about everybody knew it. He was not part of the so-called dozen. But Lazarus spent more time with Yeshu than anyone. But given his "return" {{— a dramatic return to the Jewish fold in his seventies and which was sustained to the end of his life—}} gave the new Testament redactors <now in the late part of the first century> an unforeseen

headache. Lazarus as the young companion
"back then" was just factual to all. But a full-
fledged RETURN to Judaism in the seventies
by Lazarus would damage the way these matters
concerning Lazarus could be portrayed for their
New Testament agendum. The sneaky redactors
settled on a "black-out," so to speak, of Lazarus
in his seventies. Further — just in case — the
New Testament redactors would provide a false
nomenclature for the "Lazarus" who had returned
to the fold of Judaism. They settled on "*Yokhanon/
John.*" Clever. But the Jews understood fully
what was going on. Dastardly. Dastardly, by the
"Fathers of the Church," Lazarus' true name was
displaced in the Fourth Gospel Record. His name
— for the purposes of the Fourth Gospel — was
replaced in that Gospel by cognomen: *Yokhanan/
John.* How sad and how hollow was it to pretend
that Lazarus was *Yokhanan/John*]

[[["Lazarus" tends to be the usual
nomenclature when one is speaking of
the New Testament. "Elazar" or "Eliezer"
are the nomenclatures for Lazarus when
one is speaking of the Jewish Bible.]]]

***** ***** *****

{{{Everyone knows that there was a rich man [we are speaking of sun-down on that Friday when Yeshu was crucified] who honored Yeshu by allowing Yeshu to be lied in his crypt for a time which was appropriate at that Friday at sundown. As we shall see later, the close followers of Yeshu exhumed Yeshu's body from that crypt as Friday circa mid-night became early Saturday (just after midnight). It was his half-brother [James/ *Yaakob*] who quietly brought back Yeshu's corpse to Nazareth where Yeshu belonged. This has been more dimensions to these matters in other parts of the accountings of this double *crypting*.}}}

*****

Back to 8: 13 — 58

This memorialized scene is most likely towards the end of Yeshu's public "ministry" (in a manner of speaking). It was not his first encounter with the Pharisees; not by a long shot. Indeed, this encounter was towards the end of his ministry; close to the time period constituted as that imbroglio of what that scam "Resurrection" of Lazarus who had been "buried" in the family crypt. The Bethany family was very rich and the family crypt was, so to speak, almost "comfortable." Certainly, Lazarus lost no nutrition in those four days and

three nights by virtue of the fact that Lazarus
made it clear that he had made it clear to the
servants that at the nights food and drink would
be brought over to the crypt. Further, Lazarus
made it clear that if ANY servants "squealed"
about this, ALL of the servants would be killed.
Also, the crypt was high enough so that he would
have no problem to stand up when he wanted.

This "Resurrection miracle" occurred just five
days before the "Great Shabbat" (and called the
"Great Shabbat" by virtue of the fact that it was
also the first day of *Pesakh*). The original intent
((sent in motion by Caiaphas with the "sign-off"
of Pilate)), was to radically "upgrade" the status
of this controversial figure <i.e., Yeshu>. Caiaphas
had arranged that Yeshu would be "up-graded"
so as to become the putative hero however, of
the poor and the disenfranchised. But More! He
would hold an extraordinary honor so as to be
THE HIGH PRIEST FOR THE POOR AND
DISENFRANCHISED. The hope was to siphon-
off some of the revolutionary activity which — if
not abated — would might just spark into a Revolt
against the Roman Occupation. That would be a
disaster for all. Caiaphas was throwing the dice.
The "plan" just might do the trick. After all, Yeshu
was one of them: THE DOWN-GRADED
CONDITION — DAY IN AND DAY OUT

— OF THAT HORRIBLY ONEROUS WEIGHT OF THAT HORRIBLE **ROMAN OCCUPATION.**

Caiaphas understood that a Revolt would be the worst disaster; indeed, the Temple Itself might crumble. Caiaphas understood that "The PLAN" was a long shot <which might turn into a disaster>. Caiaphas would use Yeshu's high assessment of himself. It was not clear to Caiaphas that Yeshu — who was getting attention — would be the vehicle by which this personality just might energize the lower classes with hope for a better situation despite the oneous ROMAN OCCUPATION. With this figure in the lead, Yeshu, just might electrify the leaders of the run-down population so as to follow this interesting figure who just might lessen — for the population — to put aside (for a while at least) the onerous weight of living under the Roman Occupation. Not really a revolt; just a time of some freedom and hope without a Revolt. Would it work? Probably not. But doing nothing gets you nothing.

And yet there was something about Yeshu which bothered Caiaphas.

MEDITATION THREE

Yes. Youssef claimed paternity for Yeshu. But in a small-town like Nazareth everybody knows everybody's secrets. By marrying Miriam and taking responsibility for the child, more or less, kept the *Mamzer* matter under wraps. But later, when Yeshu was no longer lodged in Nazareth and started to shake things up, the *Mamzer* matter was always brought up to haunt Yeshu, one way or another.

Also, Yeshu continued his fatal mistake by claiming for all to hear the ultimate in BLASPHEMY. To wit:

THE FATHER AND I ARE ONE

And he articulated it often; Way too often.

*****

As already noted, the Pharisees had claimed Abraham as Father. Yeshu was determined to trump Abraham. He was, so to speak, jumping off of a plane without a parachute. (In reality, he was trumping himself.)

29

Already Yeshu had flirted with another blasphemy by using a loaded grenade: **I AM <u>HE</u>**.

The syntax and the semantical input was ambiguous; but the Pharisees immediately understood the resonation. They kept up the drum-beat against this man who so often skirted blasphemy. But Yeshu was only warming up. It was not until verse 58 that sealed his fate:

I tell you most solemnly:

Before Abraham came to be.

"I AM"

He had articulated — loudly and in public — the sacred NAME. In effect, Yeshu was claiming Godhead along with "The Father."

*****   *****   *****

Now Caiaphas was not sure as to what he should do with this public blasphemy. And there had been a chance; perhaps too late. In any case, Yeshu was NOT the man for the Plan. Caiaphas — who knew everything about the planned so-called "Resurrection" of Lazarus — decided to make no decision until he could go face to face with Lazarus.*

*. {Obviously "the plan" had not addressed how radically Miriam ((not the Miriam of Yeshu}} would <u>experience</u> the putative death of her younger brother whom she adored. No one — neither or Lazarus — thought to bring Miriam into the farce. She loved her brother Lazarus above everybody in on the scam. For those three nights and four days she was anguished and kind-of "going" OUT OF HER MIND. After all, from her perspective ***LAZARUS WAS <u>ALREADY</u> DEAD!*** She could hardly drink water let alone ANY kind of food. One could claim easily that she had a TOTAL BREAKDOWN. Even when Lazarus was "resurrected" — she never returned to psychic health. It was severe. And she died soon after the trauma.}

*****   *****   *****

There was and IS but one God; period! Yeshu's claim was, just by itself, was blasphemous. By touting off the blasphemy <<***THE FATHER AND I ARE ONE***>> he put himself radically beyond the preponderance of Jews. The strict UNITY of God is the bed-rock of Judaism. The blasphemy also entailed the horrific implication that this *mamzer* was God!

The reality is that Yeshu had proclivities which were seeded in his psyche when he found, in the course of his early life, his status as a *mamzer*. He was never settled in his own skin. He wanted, desperately, to stand-out of the ordinary* <<albeit Yeshu ALREADY stood-out of the ordinary precisely in the wrong way.>>

> *. (It would be silly to point out that attitudes towards as *mamzer* in our culture are rather minor, if at all. Not so for this time period; being a *mamzer* was very notable. It was a real problem for Yeshu.)

Continuation.

He, Yeshu, DID indeed stand-out, especially when he was young. He did indeed stand out but only as he — a human like you or me — except that he indeed stood out but only insofar as he sought not normal adulation but, MORE: "over-the-top" adulation. He was not settled in his own psyche. He always wanted to be on a stage. Towards the end — but before the scam of Lazarus and Yeshu — <albeit the Pharisees largely eschewed him

except when Yeshu challenged this or that of the Pharisees>. But after what happened to Miriam, all of that *bravado* would mean NOTHING AT ALL. Please understand. There are two Miriams. The first was his mother. The other Miriam was from the Bethany family and this Miriam was central, as it turned out SO very, very badly.

In any case his drive for adulation had led him to arrange AN HYPER MIRACLE <in his mind> *SO AMAZING THAT IT WOULD EVEN CAUSE THE PHARISEES TO UNDERSTAND, FINALLY, "The father and the I are one." BUT, AS IT TURNED OUT, THAT HYPER — PUTATIVE "MIRACLE" ONLY MADE THE PHARISEES ON GUARD FIRST, AND SOME TIME LATER, OTHERS, JUST HOW TAWDRY WAS THIS SCAM RESURRECTION WAS. AND, WORSE FOR YESHU, JUST HOW BLASPHEMIC HE CAME ACROSS TO MORE AND MORE JEWS AS HE CONTINUED LOUD AND CLEAR THAT <u>HUGE</u>BLASPHEMY:*

<u>THE FATHER AND I ARE ONE</u>

*****

But, worst, of all, how these Resurection shananigans affected Miriam (of Bethany). She never recovered. This brought to Yeshu a seriousness which he lacked priorly. We shall pursue this dimension of late in life seriousness below.

*****   *****   *****   *****   *****

A REVEALING SENTMENTAL JOURNEY.
[*Matthew* 15:21] {{Matthew is on his good behavior given the aura of the journey.}

Yeshu left that place and withdrew to the region to Tyre and <u>SIDON</u>

<u>SIDON</u>; <u>SIDONIAN-ARCHER.</u>

Always and everywhere there was the missing father.

Was he alone on this journey? Another Synoptic version seems to imply that this was a sentimental journey made alone. And that would be a credible scenario given the reason for the journey in the first place. Our passage from *Matthew*, however, indicates that some of his closest followers accompanied him to this part of Israel. When there is a discrepancy between and among the synoptics, my bet would always go to the Gospel of *Matthew.** Take away the noise of the redactors from the second century *ce* of this Gospel, and one has a pretty reliable accounting of this troubled man who lived and died as a Jew. In any case, it appears that the *Matthew* document was a three year ministry condensed into one which appears to be a one year ministry.

*{{{"Matthew" may or may not be the progenitor of the text of the first Gospel.}}}

*****

The missing father. The ache which would never heal. The **Sidonian** archer who had been drafted into the Roman Army. These things were always on Yeshu's mind.

*****   *****   *****

The small military contingent, including the Archer, a Jew, who was drafted into the Roman Army. These things were always on his mind.

*****   *****   *****

So. The small military contingent, including the Archer, a Jew, in question who was forced into the Roman Army. These things were always on Yeshu's mind.

***** ***** *****

Then there is the young and beautiful maiden. She was only sixteen. Shall we call it rape? Yes maybe; No maybe. If rape means forcible intercourse with a maiden who actively resists the man's onslaught, then this was certainly rape. Is it rape if the maiden passively acquiesces to a soldier in the Roman Army? Recall Miriam (i.e., the mother of Yeshu in the future) — she was only sixteen. She lived in a small shack alone. For whatever reason she insisted on living in the small shack.

In turn, he, so to speak, bivouacked at the "Hairdreser's" home. Then there is that beautiful maiden. Again; shall we call it rape? Yes maybe; no maybe. Obviously, as above, rape means forcible intercourse with a maiden who actively resists the man's onslaught; then that would certainly be rape. Is it rape if the maiden passively acquiesces to a soldier in the Roman Army — (recall here that the whole of *YISRAEL* was under the onerous Roman Occupation)? In all of these cases so far can be made here to the effect that such is rape since the power equation favored the Archer <Pantera>. ((Of course intercourse with

36

two adults who both truly desire intercourse with each other would not — not at all — be rape.))

And there is this:

Then again, this was Miriam Magdala* ((i.e., "Hairdresser")) and the Mother of Yeshu. Such was a profession which was, to say the least, was looked upon askance.

Finally there is this: the age of the participants. Would a sixteen year old maiden who acquiesces to engage such be "off limits"?? {{Sixteen in the twenty-first century is different from sixteen back in the day.}}

Enough. What do I know?

*****

And there is this as well. Yeshu — the product of this amorous encounter by way of the Archer — was clearly the favorite of all of Miriam's children. Her first offspring <Yeshu> fathered by the Sidonian Archer. Even though he left her (he had a wife and children) very soon after the conception she fixated on the possibility that she may have conceived; and, indeed, that came to be the case.

Miriam was thrilled to have her first born by Pantera and she doted on this first-born child. Fatherless, albeit a cousin was thrilled to "father" the off-spring (albeit he was not the father). His name was Youseff. Further, Miriam knew how to make a man relish her.

Yeshu as a baby. Such a beautiful maiden and her offspring in a manner of speaking and a doting mother; and no genuine father to speak of. It is an archetype. In any case, how could Miriam feel this way of her first child if it were a forceful rape (or, for that matter, the non-forcible meaning of rape <i.e., a situation wherein the man does not use physical force over the woman but, in effect, holds some information which would be defamatory to the woman>? Perhaps she felt lucky to have her first progeny from a handsome soldier. By the standards of Nazareth Yeshu surely stood out. All this from the Sidonain Archer.

***** ***** ***** ***** *****
***** ***** *****
***** ***** ***** ***** *****

Continuing on. *Encore* and more.

Yeshu is approached by a Canaanite woman who claims her daughter is tormented by an evil spirit. Yeshu ignored her. She then intruded on

Yeshu's small group of followers to get Yeshu to do something about this woman who was causing a commotion. They, in turn, prodded Yeshu to do something about this situation. What Yeshu says here should be taken to heart for those — then as well as now — who seek about the true Yeshu: his **innate Jewishness;** and what his true self-imposed mission was all about. To his disciples and the Canaanite woman he makes it crystal clear what his calling is all about. LISTEN AND TAKE IT TO HEART!

I WAS SENT <u>ONLY</u> FOR THE LOST SHEEP OF YISRAEL

The Canaanite woman was persistent. She threw herself down and knelt before Yeshu and she begged for daughter's sake. Even then Yeshu was still resistant. Indeed, Yeshu was insulting to this frenzied woman. *LISTEN CAREFULLY. WHAT FOLLOWS REVEALS THAT YESHU'S SELF-MINISTRY **IS FOR THE JEWS AND ONLY FOR THE JEWS.*** To wit:

<u>IT IS NOT JUST TO TAKE THE CHILDREN'S FOOD AND TOSS IT TO THE HOUSE DOGS!!!</u>

YISHMAEL ben ABUYA

But her full persistence broke down Yeshu's stern demeanor and Yeshu did what he did because of the mother's persistence and her faith. The child ended up being cured.

MEDITATION FOUR

Perhaps he just wanted to die.

Friday when Yeshu was crucified, Yeshu could have "saved" himself that prior night had he simply acquiesced to the clever phrasing by Caiaphas whereby Caiaphas phrased the charge in such a way that Yeshu — had he not been in his own death spiral — could have easily crafted an answer would exculpate him. But Yeshu, by this time, wanted to die. He sealed his chosen fate by once more — and LOUD — claiming ALOUD with the one answer which would GUARENTEE his own death. He started in with the SACRED FOUR-LETTER name of God <<*yud hey vav hey*>> from 3:14 of EXODUS followed by — yet again claiming that — *"THE FATHER AND I ARE ONE"*!!!! *EITHER of these blasphemies would be a supreme and unforgivable blasphemy.* Either one would set in motion for a death penalty; Yeshu had — probably in purpose — TWO reasons for setting up for a Blasphemy trial.

Caiaphas now realized that — unless this Yeshu guy would relent his blasphemy ((but such did not happen)) at the last straw — he would suffer the death sentence. Yeshu would not reject his blasphemy. The reality is that it became clear that Yeshu WANTED TO DIE. Since this blasphemer would not back down on his public and egregiously blasphemic claims, Caiaphas had no other option than to bring about a death writ against Yeshu. Again, however, even religious matters involving a death penalty had to be adjudicated by Pilate.

Of course Pilate didn't care a whit about blasphemy. Caiaphas' concern — now that the Plan had been blown to smithereens by Yeshu — was centered on the apparent messianic dimensions of this crazy Jew. For under the strictures of the Occupation, a fair amount of Jews maintained that the Messiah would be a military figure who would inspire a rebellion against the Roman Occupation.

Pilate himself had been, initially, "charmed," so to speak, by this crazy Jew who was to have been the lynch-pin of the Plan. << The "Plan">> Caiaphas had used Yeshu for his purposes who <i.e., Yeshu> in turn WAS quite proud to take center stage. But it became clear to Pilate that Yeshu had now totally rejected his critical role in "The Plan" by virtue of Yeshu's curious (i.e., curious now to Pilate) change of heart predicated on Yeshu's life-changing encounter with Miriam at Bethany. <<<It is not impossible that the very NAME, *MIRIAM*, <i.e., the Miriam from Bethany> conjured up conscious and unconscious emotions associate with his own doting mother name *MIRIAM*.>>>

In any case, Yeshu was interrogated by Pilate with regard to the putative Messianic aura of this spell-binding figure who now wanted nothing else than to die. Now that the ""Plan" had been blown sky-high, Pilate had to be assured that his charismatic dreamer — if freed — would NOT set in motion a Rebellion against the Occupation with Yeshu playing the role of a usurping Messiah. Pilate attributed way too much concern with regard to Yeshu who, now, only wanted to die.

Long story short: Pilate tried every which way to get this troubled dreamer to eschew Messianic Rebellion. But Pilate couldn't get a straight answer from this strange Nazarene even though Rebellion by way of Yeshu was simply ridiculous. Pilate couldn't fathom that Yeshu — at this point. What Pilate could not fathom was that Yeshu

YISHMAEL ben ABUYA

WANTED nothing but TO BE killed since it would be wrong for himself to kill himself.

*****   *****   *****

Now imagine this. It is November 22 of 1963; and nothing was said about these matters. No newspapers reports; no radio or TV reports. **Nothing at all!**

The analogy is, of course, very imprecise and imperfect. But it gets the idea across graphically. ALL THREE OF THE SYNOPTICS PASS OVER THIS **MOST PROMINENT** OF ALL THE WORDS AND ACTIONS OF YESHU'S **THREE-YEAR** MINISTRY: Such is, just by itself, an indictment of the Synoptics.* And, in the final analysis, this suppression turned out not to be drum tight. TRUTH CAN be successfully suppressed for long periods of time. But in some canny way, TRUTH does find a way to make itself known. TRUTH does find a way to make itself known. Yes; incrementally and by *innuendo*. YES INDEED!

> *. Year after Year; Decade after Decade; stalwarts breeze by the INCREDIBLE *mish/mosh* of life and nothing happens. I chose here to

44

emphasize the radical INCONGRUITY of and between the Synoptics and the Gospel called "John." To be sure, there are two layers of that Fourth Gospel: the original early version penned by Lazarus soon after Yeshu died; and — almost a century later — the Hellenic over-wash orchestrated by our early "Fathers of the Church."

One must travel through this Fourth Gospel for some time in order to delineate the true original early version penned by Lazarus <at least the portions which were allowed by those early "Fathers of the Church">. But towards the end of the first century the "Fathers of the Church" would allow the Lazarus production to have a place at the table for the Lazarus document only on the condition that much of the Lazarus production is suppressed. More than that, those "wonderful" *(sic)* Fathers of the Church intruded with an Hellenic overlay which would portray Yeshu as something he wasn't AT ALL: a Greeky/ Hellenic <false> Yeshu. Those who knew better are able to tract the portions — the remaining ones since those "Fathers" had intruded into Lazarus's manuscript — the Lazarus portions and leave the rest for the uneducated.

Time takes Time. There is, even now, some possibility will expand which will put forth more about the Lazarus Document.

What I am writing is more than *innuendo*. However, most likely this revelation (and for that matter, this long production in which this scandal is ensconced) will not be read at all or read and simply dismissed. Time takes Time.

*****   *****   *****   *****   *****

MEDITATION FIVE

But again, and to his credit, in those last days, Yeshu comported himself in such a way that he — and only he — would pay the price for the fraud. But that is only one side of the story.

So yes, Matthew's *ur*-document was the template for the other two Synoptics <even though Matthew knew what he had suppressed>. Also, Matthew was one who came to sense that this man, Yeshu, was more than a fraud. He, Mathew, decided to create a document which put forth the better and stirring dimensions of this "Yeshu" despite knowing the VERY substantial negative dimensions of Yeshu.

It was a terrible mistake. Rivers of blood — mostly Jewish — flowed because of Matthew's suppression. And worse — WAY worse — **not truthful**. For the suppression kept the radically flawed dimensions of Yeshu under wraps. {{OR, Matthew DID include the drama of the Lazarus fraud-resurrection — AND THEN IT WAS SUPPRESSED.}} My own bet is that early <<i.e., prior to the emergence of the fourth Gospel

47

circa 100/125>> Christian redactors "cleaned" this embarrassing "chapter" in Yeshu's "life" albeit he was long buried by this time. In any case, it was Matthew's Gospel which took the lead in suppressing from his document what was the scandalous "Resurrection." Both Mark and Luke continued their suppressing of the scam Resurrection from Matthew's lead *or having the suppression by those "Fathers of the church suppressed suck."

*****   *****   *****

Back in Nazareth Joseph produced two more male offspring by way of Miriam. Soon after Joseph died. His brother took over Joseph's offspring with Miriam and produced two or three more offspring from Miriam. Both of them were good fathers. But always the first-born from Pantera held her heart.

And, when Yeshu found out who his father was Yeshu was confused. It was good for Yeshsu to have found out who was his father. Yet, as he started to know dimensions of Pantera, it hurt Yeshu to find out that Pantera stayed only three days after the conception. He left baby Yeshu without knowing whether his Mother had conceived or not. From that time Yeshu — consciously and unconsciously — Pantera was in his brain. And it was no accident that in his roamings Yeshu managed to frequent the area of ***SIDON***.

***** ***** ***** ***** *****

Continuing on.

Yeshu now came to fully understand that his "resurrection miracle" was in fact his death warrant. To Yeshu's benefit he made it understood that Yeshu now comported himself such that he — and ONLY he — would take on the burden of such a blasphemy <i.e., that crazy resurrection scam> along with the even greater blasphemy whereby Yeshu proclaimed several times (and with witnesses) that "THE FATHER AND I ARE ONE."

Further, to credit Yeshu's concern for Lazurus, keep in mind that he, Yeshu, counseled Lazarus to become unavailable and holed up in his family's home. It was the Wednesday prior to that "Holy Thursday" and things would tight. {However, Lazarus did not follow Yeshu on this matter.}

It became more certain that Yeshu would be charged with blasphemy one way or another. It was important, however, that the charge NOT be, initially, the charge of blasphemy. Caiaphas understood that Blasphemy is not something that Pilate would allow as a capital offence. He would not bring up the Blasphemy matter until the matters important to Pilate were adjudicated. At that point it would be Caiaphas who would deal with the Blasphemy matter <albeit, it would not be by "hanging from a tree" as *per* Jewish Law>. For Caiaphas the charge of blasphemy* was the main thing even if the form of execution would not be "hanging from a tree." Indeed this blasphemy business was just jerky from Pilate's perspective

But back, now, the matters of Pilate's Messianic maters had to be adjudicated before the Jewish Blasphemy matter could be taken care of. Caiaphas molded the two matters together.

Hanging from a tree was out of the question <albeit in Jewish concerns "hanging from a tree" was the *kosher* way of taking out a Blasphemer>. Pilate would laugh in Caiaphas' face if Caiaphas brought up the "hanging from a tree" matter. So Caiaphas worked on what was possible so that a blasphemer would suffer the death penalty, one way or another.*

*. Near Two millennia of Judaism had transpired from this time involving Yeshu, Caiaphas, and Pilate. To the best of my knowledge Jewish Law does not now make Blasphemy a capital offence albeit it is still an offence especially with regard to articulating the sacred **NAME of GOD**.

Given this Roman Occupation <<let us not forget that all this transpired in Israel; an Israel which, sadly, had to deal Jewish sacred matters according to the whims of Pilate>> there could only be a proxy capital offence according to Roman Law and NOT — under the conditions which obtained then — Jewish Law. Caiaphas orchestrated this tightrope matter. What did he come up with? It was indeed ludicrous, but such is the sorrow of being Occupied in your own land.

Insurrection was the main problem according Pilate. Caiaphas orchestrated a claim of INSURRECTION <which caught Pilate's ear and eye>. OF COURSE IT WAS A FABRICATON. But Jewish justice would not allow for a blasphemy in the very Land of Israel <albeit Occupied>. So justice required that the Jewish blasphemer be subjected to the death penalty by proxy of ROMAN LAWS OF INSURRECTION!

The charge of being a Moshiach/Messiah was usually, then, understood as a military figure for the Israelites. In other words, the Roman Law had no concern with the blasphemies of those crazy Jews. But Caiaphas in cahoots with Pilate had arranged that the crime would not be held according to the Jewish Blasphemy codes but rather according to Roman Laws of INSURRECTION. Imagine that!

So the matter of Yeshu would fall under the ROMAN Laws of INSURRECTION on two charges: The first claim is that Yeshu maintained that with the help of the "Father" the HUGE TEMPLE WOULD BE DESTROYED. The second matter would be the multiple ways of disrupting the inter-changing of money people like Yeshu who actually upended the table of a money-changer thereby upending the money place of working. <<There is some weight on this second charge since the money changers were akin to our banks.>> In any case, Yeshu was doing nothing at all to save himself and nor to admit fault where there was fault.

Of course, the other charge was bogus: *With the help of the Father the **HUGE TEMPLE WOULD BE DESTROYED!*** This second charge, of course, was bogus. But the two charges together — one bogus and one fair — had some weight; but certainly not necessarily to the point of being executed. In any case, the whole thing was somewhat ludicrous; anyway you cut it all you would have to was to just LOOK: This man was no "insurrectionist." But the charges were enough since Yeshu himself did nothing for himself; he WANTED to die. <and he did>

*****

Yeshu was putty in Caiaphas' hands. When the time came, Pilate "washed his hands" with regard to Yeshu. Yeshu's fate was now in the hands of Caiaphas. The charges said what they said. But the charges did not really get to the blasphemy matter.

So Caiaphas ((for the record since Yeshu was already from Caiaphas' viewpoint a blasphemer)) stood on the "verdict" and put forth the charge of blasphemy <<over and above the two indictments of INSURRECTION>>.

Caiaphas, for the record, orchestrated Yeshu to own **the gross Blasphemy FOR YEARS** indictment claiming that "The Father and I are One." "If you need to say such, do such

by yourself" was the attitude. Children will get
the idea and turn children to be not sure that
what their parents told them. That is wrong
and confusing to young children who hear
from a substantial figure like Yeshu preaching a
BLASPHEMY. That is wrong.

One way or another, Yeshu — in that ambiance
— Yeshu had to die for the sake of trashing of the
most fundamental caveat of Jewish LAW: THE
SACRED UNITY OF GOD in Judaism. And,
in fact, what Yeshu WAS, by now, proclaiming
his **VARIENCE!!!** of JEWISH LAW* <<which
was, in fact, going against the unity of the
SACRED UNITY OF GOD in Judaism.>>.
That's all that Caiaphas would need to bring this
whole matter to a death warrant, so to speak;
And it did.

> *.   {Obviously   Yeshu's   continued
> BLASPHEMY is, *eo ipso,* insofar that Yeshu's
> compunction to and for his blasphemy **IS**,
> *of itself,* **A MAJOR CONTRADICTION
> OF THE UNITY OF GOD in Judaism.**}

***** ***** ***** ***** *****
***** ***** *****
***** ***** ***** ***** *****

54

{{Lazarus took it upon himself to be involved in what was to be the last two days of Yeshu even though Yeshu tried to persuade him to stay in his home.}}

*****

This claim "THE FATHER AND I ARE ONE", would be — and was — <**AND IS**> just about the worst blasphemy possible. Ever since the false resurrection (((along with the fact that most <but certainly not all> understood that the "glorious resurrection" was but a stupid scam))) Yeshu was already subdued. Miriam's <i.e., the sister of Lazarus> reaction to the false "resurrection" — ORCHESTRATED BY YESHU ***AND HER OWN BELOVED BROTHER*** — went into an emotional tailspin from which she would never recover. Yes. Yeshu himself wept uncontrollably for her and he understood that, ultimately, Miriam, the sister of Lazarus — who ***adored both Lazarus and Yeshu*** — could never recover. She retreated into herself and died VERY young.*

> *. The mordent *"Yeshu Wept"* of JOHN* 11:36 is the greatest example of *litotes* in the whole of Western Literature.

**. Those "Fathers of the Church" used the name "John"/*Yochanan* as the identity of the original original fourth Gospel. It was a dodge. They simply would not allow the true name of the lion's share of the fourth Gospel to be Lazarus.

They knew that Lazarus (i.e., *Elazar/Eliezer)* was the true pen for the first and true writing of the initial writing of the fourth Gospel. As we have seen below, the "ever" invasive "Fathers of the Church" kind of ruined the initial version with that Hellenic intrusion into the Gospel. But the true Fourth Gospel was the one scripted by Lazarus despite those intrusions into the original. And Jews could sense out the portions of the Lazarus manuscript while skipping over the other Hellenic sorry story.

***** ***** ***** ***** *****
***** ***** *****
***** ***** ***** ***** *****

But again, and to his credit, in those last days, Yeshu comported himself in such a way that he — and only he — would pay the price for the fraud. But that is only one side of the story.

*****

56

So yes. Matthew's *ur*-document was the template for the other two Synoptics <even though Matthew's *ur*— document was the template for the other two Synoptics though Matthew knew what he had surpressed>. Also, Matthew was one who came to sense that this man, Yeshu was more than a fraud. He, Matthew, decided to create a document which put forth the better and stirrings of this "Yeshu" even knowing the VERY substantial negative dimensions of Yeshu.

It was a terrible mistake. Matthew only brought out the "good Yeshu." The other side of Yeshu was carefully put aside. Rivers of blood — mostly Jewish — flowed because of Matthew's suppression; and worse — WAY worse — **not truthful**. For the suppression kept radically flawed dimensions of Yeshu under wraps. {{OR, Matthew DID include the drama of the Lazarus/Yeshu resurrection — AND THEN IT WAS SUPPRESSED <by those New Testatment redactors>}}. My own bet is that early <i.e., prior to the emergence of the fourth Gospel circa 100/125> Christian redactors "cleaned" this embarrassing "chapter" <i.e., the resurrection fraud> in Yeshu's life. In any case it was Matthew's Gospel which took the lead in suppressing from his document what the truth was about the scandalous "Resurrection." Both

Luke and Mark continued their suppressing of the Resurrection following the lead of Matthew.

*****   *****   *****

Back in Nazareth Joseph produced two more male offspring by way of Miriam. Soon after Joseph died. His brother took over Joseph's offspring with Miriam and produced two or three more offspring from Miriam. Both of them were good fathers. But always the first born from Pantera held her heart.

And, when Yeshu found out who his father was Yeshu was confused. It was good for Yeshu to have found out who was his father. Yet, as he started to begin to know dimensions of Pantera, it hurt Yeshu that Pantera stayed with Yeshu's mother for only three days. He left baby Yeshu without even knowing whether his Mother had conceived or not. From that time — consciously and unconsciously — Pantera was always in his brain.

*****

Eventually, over the next century, Matthew's document — and its two imitations with slightly differing agenda — fell into the hands of a generation filled with hate because — putatively — "Jews" rejected Yeshu as the Messiah. ((Given the life of Yeshu it would be suicidal and **farcical** at once for the "Jews" to even consider to 'crown', so to speak, someone like Yeshu.))

Again, in any case over that next century, Matthew's document — and its two imitations with slightly differing agenda — fell into the hands of a generation filled with hate because — putatively — "Jews" rejected Yeshu as the Messiah. That generation ((and such characterizes MANY Christians to this day)) had **<and still today>** had the thinnest understanding of that troubled man, Yeshu. The final version of Matthew's "*ur*-document" contained MANY omissions while it sanitized some of Yeshu's deep shortcomings. Especially his famous Blasphemy which brought him to the crucifixion.

All three of the Synoptics suffered, over time, by Christian redactional "expansions" <and some matters of deletion>. Keep this in mind: Those "Fathers of the Church" tended to delete some passages which — in their emphasizes and/ or deletions which either demeaned the Jewish dimension of Yeshu and/or suppressing: *just how Jewish he was: JEWISH TO THE VERY MARROW OF HIS BONES!*: EXACTLY

YISHMAEL ben ABUYA

WHAT THOSE FATHERS DIDN'T WANT TO KNOW.

```
*****   *****   *****   *****   *****
*****   *****   *****
*****   *****   *****   *****   *****
```

Insertion:

Generally speaking QABBALA is not really based on anything in Scripture. Keep that in mind: **Most of Qabbalah is insipid and not worthy to stand in the company of Jews.** However, QABBALA, as we shall see, puts forth a curious teaching which, I aver — and despite the over-riding shallowness of "QABBALA" in general — allows for **AN** insight to the deepest holiness of Judaism. Such is this paradox. Just listen before you walk away.

The emergence of QABBALA in Provence in the late eleventh and early twelth centuries. Such was picked up by a clever and poetic Spanish Jew <with a nagging wife to boot>, Moses de Leon, who finally settled upon the Tanna, Shimon bar Yokai, as his main puppet <so to speak> protagonist for his writings. Moses committed his lively ruminations to writing and the product was *THE ZOHAR*. Then, as the **ZOHAR** wafted over the Mediterranean Sea, it found its home in Tsaft, one of the four holy cities. There was a shy scholar, Isaac Luria, who eschewed committing his thoughts in writing, brought to consciousness orally, a teaching which — ***despite*** its pedigree in Qabbalaism — hearkened back to the notes on the WORK OF CREATION of another shy Rabbi, "Ben Zoma" back in the time of the Tannaim. This teaching was the *tsimtsum* teaching in concert called "the breaking of the vessels."

Our shy protagonist talked about these adventures of the mind to a very few limited set of people, one of them of which, Rabbi Khaiyam Vitale, who had taken notes after the sessions with Rabbi Luria. These esoteric teachings started to germinate in a small group who "signed up" for this fantasmagoric journey of the mind. Later, *Baal Shem Tov* pursued these Lurianic adventures by way of the saved writings of Rabbi Khaiyim. And finally we arrive at the appearance of the one who dared to correct his mentor, Rabbi Luria (((i.e., not in the flesh, to be sure, but way tales and certain writings <Vitale's notes in particular>))). His name was (and is):

NA Nakh Nakhman Nakhman b-Uman

And it was this man who brought Qabbala to the point wherein this totally-extrinsic-to-Scripture undertaken of several centuries came to bend back on itself producing in the process the secrets of *Ben Zoma* if you can find them). I am speaking of the great understanding of the *tsimtsum* teaching, initiated by Luria and brought to full fruition by our Bratslaver Rebbe.

For all practical purposes the *Siferot*; the "ineffable One"; and its offspring theology which is often referred to as ***via negativa theology***; and, of course, the putative **"AYN-SOF"** ———— VIRTUALLY ALL OF THAT IS FOREIGN TO TRUE JUDAISM. What is left over is the pearl: the *tsitsum* of Luria as corrected by Rabbi Nakhman. This last is truly the secret (albeit not yet fully acknowledged); and this pearl is QUITE SEPARABLE from the "bells and whistles" of the *siferot; the "Ineffable One; the* via negative *theology*; and that contrived trope **"AYN-SOF"** *whether it is deployed by Moses ben Maimon or by the Qabbalists}* This whole charade is but Hebraized Neo-Plotonianism spruced-up with Neo-Pythagoreanism.

The pearl, however, is a different matter. It can, does, ***and should,*** stand by itself. Indeed, the pearl (i.e., the *tsimtsum* teaching of Rabbi Luria corrected by Rabbi Nakhman)* is properly respected ONLY when it is divorced from all those bells and whistles which people call "Qabbalah."

> *. {{Luria understood that the __outward contracting__ by God creates a space **WHICH IS** incongruous insofar that there would be a place ***UTTERLY BEREFT OF GO!!!*** Accordingly, Rabbi Luria postulated that somewhere there was some *"reshimu" of light* <i.e., some weak of presence of God even in that space which was *supposed* to be utterly empty>. But in so doing Luria missed the deeper — and darker — revelation.
>
> It took the mind and heart of Rabbi Nakhman to endorse the full import of Rabbi's initial (and faulty) revelation. The true — albeit uncanny — reality such that ***tsimtsum* REALLY DOES CREATE A SPACE — A "MAQOM" — *WHICH IS UTTERLY BEREFT OF GOD.*** {follow carefully here} This utterly uncanny *"MAQOM"* is the *NOT-GOD* **OF** **GOD.** It turns out that the utterly uncanny **"MAQOM"** is more

than God since absent **"MAQOM"**
there is no God.}}

*****   *****   *****

To close this out: TAKE NOTE: *Pace Luria
and Nakhman,* **QABBALA HAS VIRTUALLY
NOTHING TO DO WITH OUR JEWISH
REVELATION. IT IS SPAWNED FROM
"Neo-Platonism *AND NOT* FROM OUR
SCRIPTURE.**

Insert Finished.

*****   *****   *****   *****   *****

**When pre-existing Theology interferes with
the natural meaning of Scripture <Jewish
Scripture> it only means that the Theology is
defective.**

MEDITATION SIX

When pre-existing Theology interferes with the natural meaning of Scripture <Jewish Scripture> **it only means that the Theology is defective.**

*****   *****   *****

When Yeshu arrived at Jerusalem from Bethany he was a changed man and no-longer interested in "The Plan."

*****

Some time later the ROMAN OCCUPATION CAME TO BE **SO ONEROUS** that the population SUDDENLY CHALLENGED THE OCCUPATION. For a while the Jewish population actually had some successes. But ROME would not allow such. The Revolt was decimated. "Rivers" of Jewish blood. This time <<circa the end of "bc" and the beginning of "ad"; (OF COURSE) those were not the markers actually used back then>>. ROME allowed this polity this time to continue <albeit totally in the grip of ROME.>

But the Jews got antsy about seventy years later and decided to expel the Roman Occupation. The Jews again took on the Roman Occupation {circa 68 — 73 *ad*} and actually expelled the Romans from the land. Just for a while. When Rome came back it was more bloody for the Jews; worse than what transpired about seventy years earlier. But Jerusalem was wasted including the Temple.*

> *. The notable Rabbis took refuge to the small area of YAVNE. It became the unofficial "capital" of the Jews. Much Scripture work was achieved at Yavne. But time and 'wind' took its own ravishment.

It is one thing to be the loser of a revolutionary outbreak. But it was Aqiba who forced a MAJOR show-down about seventy years into the new millennium. For a relatively short time — we are speaking of months — Rome actually withdrew. But ROME could not allow such a small country as Israel to be vindicated. Rome eventually returned and *utterly decimated the Jewish Polity.* For all purposes its great and grand Temple was gutted. Yes; there was the Western Wall. But there was no Temple to speak of.

It's one thing to be a polity even when Occupied. It is quite another story to be a polity which came to be *utterly decimated*. It was AQIBA who coached the Jews to take up arms against an enemy many times stronger than the Jewish Polity. It would be almost nineteen centuries before the Jews themselves — with vicious enemies on all sides — re-instated Israel as a polity in 1947.

```
*****   *****   *****   *****   *****
*****   *****   *****
*****   *****   *****   *****   *****
```

To Miriam <the brother of Lazarus> the three nights and four days were excruciating for Lazarus' sister. So, then, when Yeshu arrived at Jerusalem from the disaster at Bethany he was a changed man and no-longer interested in "The Plan." This has been explained in detail elsewhere in this production. In any case, Caiaphas was worried. The initial reports from Bethany indicated that Yeshu had a radical change. He certainly was no longer the man who — with the major help of Lazarus — was to "up-grade" his status *visa vis* the people. All in all the so-called Resurrection was a farce, and, eventually, everybody knew it. But *that* Yeshu was now no-more than a "dead-man-walking."

To make matters worse, Lazarus and Yeshu had failed to bring Miriam <Lazarus's older sister who adored her younger brother> into the fraud Resurrection. <<There was, also, another sister, Martha, who seemed, right from the beginning that Yeshu "was off.">>

Those four days and three nights when Lazarus ((thinking he was dead all the while)) was entombed took the spirit from her in a way which would never be the same. THEN to see the scam "resurrection" wherein Lazarus came out of the tomb knowing that he was perpetrating a scam with Yeshu, the masterminds of the whole miserable scene. It was more than Miriam could shoulder. The younger sister had **really** <u>**experienced**</u> her beloved brother's DEATH. And now she was experiencing her own — slower — death. It really was too much for her. She couldn't eat and barely sip water. Something like a death while breathing <and not breathing by much>. She never recovered.

What Miriam went through changed everything for Yeshu. He now understood just how stupid he, Yeshu, was. Now he wanted nothing more than a "dead man walking." He wanted to die. And he wanted to die in such a way that Lazarus would come out alright. This was, after all, the scheme was to radically "upgrade" Yeshu's standing so as to convince the people that this man was more than just a man. The whole thing was baloney and now he knew it; he birthed this nonsense. Indeed Yeshu was a truly a "dead man walking." He wouldn't resist that new-to-him manner of being. Now he really WANTED no more than being "a dead man walking."

*****   *****   *****

Now back to some of the earlier dimensions.

The bottom line was this: On the one hand, as we have seen, Yeshu acknowledged that the Pharisees took it upon their-selves to maintain a greater effort for the *Halakha* compared to those — like Yeshu — with his concern limited to the *Mitsvot* of Scripture. ((Of course the Pharisees followed the *Mitsvot* of Scripture.)). Yet from time to time Yeshu was careful to maintain that *de facto,* the Pharisees took upon their more requisites because of their belief in the Oral Torah —— something which has **NO Scriptural validation AT ALL**. This was a concern for Yeshu. And indeed, the Oral Torah — which is the well, so to speak — for a BIG *Halakha*. But The attitude was that it was not that important to validate what should and should not be put into the *Halakha* without trying to find in Scripture for the ever blossoming of Oral Torah "findings" all over the place without checking out with Scripture.

Accordingly, Yeshu praised this undertaking* by the Pharisees whereby they took on a wider set of requirements for themselves <albeit, these "extras" were not maintained in Scripture.> All in all, however, there remained tension on this matter and other matters which kept Yeshu and other Scripture-centric believers at odds on this matter. Now and then it would flare up in a controversy.

> *. Yes. The Pharisees expanded the domain for the Pharisaic invention. On the one hand Yehsu would note that it was worthy, for the Pharisees, to expand the set of requirements to be brought into the *Halakha*. However, Yesh made it clear that this expansion **violates a fundamental understanding to the effect that ANY expansion is valid if and only if the putative expansion is found in Scripture; and that was the case here.** In other words the Pharisees were generating mandates WITHOUT VALIDATION IN SCRIPTURE.

The paragraph just above stands. But there was another — and more consequential — "bone in the throat."; a big one. There was something OF MUCH WEIGHTY MATTERS which dwarfed the intramural charges and counter charges of and by the two groupings. However, far and away, these "normal" differences with respect to the *Halakha* was transcended by Yeshu's stubborn and blasphemous refrain. The refrain was a straight-out BLASPHEMY. Not just once, but in other venues as well. And then there was the huge *and weighty* bombshell <given in this somber and Holy ambiance>: Yeshu and his treasured Blasphemy for all to hear on that Holy Thursday. Further, his articulation was such that there could be no possibility of ambiguity. To wit:

THE FATHER AND I ARE ONE

***** ***** ***** ***** *****

***** ***** *****

***** ***** ***** ***** *****

Continuing on: The Pharisaic Invention of the Oral Torah.

Protocols had to be brought into being for dealing with not only the original *Mistvot* of Scripture BUT

71

ALSO—when and as the new kid on the block <i.e., the Pharisees> invented Oral Torah *halakhot*— it came to be the case that there had to be protocols for those putative Oral 'enactments' for both the *Mitsvot* of Scripture **and** those putative Oral Torah *halakhot*. However, **such**protocols, initially, **were not at all treated in <u>any way at all</u> as** *halakhot* **and** *a-fortiori,* **NOT to be treated as Scriptural** *Mitsvot.*

***** ***** *****

But circumstances changed, especially by virtue of the ascendency of the Pharisaic Sect. The Pharisaic Sect was in ascendency while the Scripture/Tsadduqeans (a Sect, most probably, which had its genesis from the *SOFERIM*) were struggling to have that kind of influence in *Beit Yisrael.*

And here is the last chapter on this sad development.

In addition to those Oral Torah *halakhot* ((all, <u>allegedly</u>, from the mouth of Hashem at Sinai and then passing them on <<getting more numerous each year>> from generation to generation)) the Pharisaic Sect (and their heirs in the Rabbinic Movement) actually started to "upgrade" the status of these *takannot/Enactments* virtually to the level of Oral Torah *halakhot*. This "upgrading" came to have a status and a heading: "Rabbinic Enactments"/ *"takanot."*

For this Purpose they counted those more advanced *"takanot"* [along with virtually anything else which they wished to "upgrade"] as, virtually, true *halakhot*. Pretty soon the Pharisaic **and their heirs even unto our time** <i.e., most of Orthodoxy with the exception of "Modern Orthodox"> came awash with *Mitsvot;* the putative Oral Torah *halakhot*; and the caveats of Rabbinic Enactments, all of which <i.e., except for the *Mitsvot* of Scripture> exponentially grew and continued to grow. It reminds me of Scripture in the sense that Scripture does not expand; there is and should be there are healthy limits. But the Pharisees went on in there expansive (and putative) merry way of an expansive Oral Torah (which, you will remember NEVER HAD SCRIPTURE JUSTIFICATION for those putative Oral Torah mandates from Sinai in the first place only to create mountains of putative Oral Torah mandates. And it continues.

What started out as a set of common-sense protocols for the implementing (and sometimes suspending) the *Mitsvot* of Scripture came to morph into a bloated "Halakha." Such is unhealthy in several ways including something like a *downgrading* of that part of spirituality which is joined at the hip with the *Halakha*. Please don't get me wrong. An assiduous commitment to the "*Halakha*" is **ep ipso** spiritual. But such is not the whole of spirituality.

***** ***** *****
*****
***** ***** *****

Again for the record:

The mordent 'Yeshu wept' of 'John 11:36' when the 'Resurrection' revealed is the greatest example of litotes *in the whole Western Literature.*

***** ***** *****

The sparring between the Pharisees and Yeshu was intense. In the earlier years of his ministry the interchanges between Yeshu and the Pharisees were more like sparring under the same umbrella rather than being straight-out enemies. Recall here that the Synoptic accounting of the ministry was put forth, foolishly, as a one-year affair. By compressing almost three years into one, the effect of each of these overlapping narratives were sudden, falsely dramatic, and poorly condensed. The reality is that the Fourth Gospel was way more true to the historical situation. But, over time and incrementally, Yeshu became more presumptuous about his (putative) standing with God and with *Beit Israel.* In his third year, Yeshu bandied his "cane" <so to speak> by bandying his "treasure":

THE FATHER AND I ARE ONE

For him, it was his staff. For virtually all others it was a Blasphemy. We shall pick up the journey in its third year roughly a couple of weeks before the (so-called) "resurrection." To wit:

The refrain was a straight-out BLASPHEMY. Not just once, but in other venues as well. And then there were the huge <u>and weighty</u> bombshells <given in this somber and HOLY ambiance>. Yeshu and his treasured BLASPHEMY for all to hear on that Holy Thursday.

Further, his articulation was such that there could be no possibility of ambiguity. To wit: loud and gusty:

THE FATHER AND I ARE ONE

YISHMAEL ben ABUYA

There will be more forthcoming on this matter.

*****   *****   *****   *****   *****
*****   *****   *****
*****   *****   *****   *****   *****

Continuing on: The Pharisaic Invention of the Oral Torah.

Protocols had to be brought into being for dealing with not only the original *Mitsvot* of Scripture BUT ALSO — when and as the new kid on the block \<the Pharisees\> invented Oral Torah *halakhot* — it came to be the case that there had to be protocols for those putative 'enactments' for both the *Mitsvot* of Scripture **and** those putative Oral Torah *halakhot*. However, **such** *protocols,* initially, **were not at all to be treated in any way at all** *as halakhot and* **a fortiori, NOT at all to be treated as Scriptural** *Mitsvot*.

*****   *****   *****

But circumstances changed, especially by virtue of the ascendency of the Pharisaic Sect. The Pharisaic Sect was in ascendency while the Scripture/Tsadduqeans (a Sect, most probably, which had its genesis from the *SOFERIM*) were

76

struggling to have that kind of influence in *Beit Yisrael.*

And here is the last chapter on this sad development:

In addition to those Oral Torah *halakhot* ((all allegedly from the mouth of H̲ashem at Sinai and then passing them on <<getting more numerous each year>> from generation to generation>> the Pharisaic Sect (and their heirs in the Rabbinic Movement) actually started to "upgrade" the status of these *takannot/Enactments* virtually to the level of Oral Torah *halakhot.* This "upgrading" came to have a status and a heading: "Rabbinic-Enactments/*takanot.*" For this purpose they counted those more advanced *takanot* [along with virtually anything else which they wished to "upgrade"] as, virtually, true *halakhot.* Pretty soon the Pharisaic Sect ***and their heirs even unto our time*** <most of Orthodoxy with the exception of the Modern Orthodox> came awash with *Mitsvot; the putative Oral Torah* halakhot; *and the caveats of Rabbinic Enactments,* all of which <except for the *Mitsvot* of Scripture> exponentially grew and continued to grow. It reminds of cancer. What started out as a set of common-sense protocols for the implementing (and sometimes suspending) the *Mitsvot* of Scripture came to morph into a bloated "Halakha." Such is unhealthy in several ways including something like a *downgrading* of that part of spirituality which is joined at the hip with the *Halakha*.

Please don't get me wrong. An assiduous commitment to the "**Halakha**" is **eo ipso** spiritual. But such is not the whole of spirituality.

***** ***** *****

Again for the record:

The mordent "Yeshu wept" of John 11:36 *is the greatest example of* litotes *in the whole of Western Literature.*

***** ***** *****

The sparring between of the Pharisees and Yeshu was intense. In the earlier years of his ministry the interchanges between Yeshu and the Pharisees were more like sparring under the same umbrella rather than being straight-out enemies. [[[Recall here that the Synoptic accounting of the ministry of Yeshu was a one-year affair. By compressing almost three years into one, the effect of each of these overlapping narratives was sudden, dramatic, *and poorly condensed.* The reality is that the Fourth Gospel was way more true to the historical situation than the Synoptics.]]] But, over time and incrementally, Yeshu became more and more presumptuous about his (putative) standing with God and with *Beit Yisrael*. We shall pick up the journey in its third year roughly a couple of weeks before the (so-called) "Resurrection" of Lazarus.

MEDITATION SEVEN

Excepting Yeshu's banding around his horrible blasphemy towards the ending of the third year of Yeshu's "ministry" ————— the tension of and between Yeshu and the Pharisees remained relatively always as an INTRAMURAL matter **WITHIN JUDAISM**. The **fabricated** Yeshu of the Synoptics is NOT true. Once again, we must remind ourselves that the figure of Yeshu in the Synoptics ——— {{{{after all, those "Fathers of the Church" stilted the Jewish reality and demeanor in favor of a "cleaned up" <from their perspective> accounting of these things even to the extent that such could present a non-Jewish flavor to this Yeshu of the Synoptics.!!!!!}}}} ——— is nothing more than the power of those "Fathers of the Church" to frame these matters **such that one might think that Yeshu was a Christian!!!!!! Dirty work, indeed.**

Once again we must remind ourselves that the figure of Yeshu in the Synoptics is, simply, the Yeshu who died on the cross and was FULLY JEWISH. Yes; it is true. As it became clear that the non-Jews were taking over what became more and more a non-Jewish gathering and which was becoming an Hellenic affair orchestrated by the Church Fathers which would — if Yeshu were still alive and he was not — be radically foreign to Yeshu. If Yeshu "returned" to the earth <so to speak> ((and he hasn't and he will not)) no-one would recognize the true Yeshu. The charming creation of "Jesus" for followers of Yeshu who were/are English had nothing at all real *vis a vis* the real flesh and blood of the actual **JEWISH** Yeshu; not even close.

In any case, the gentiles also started to take notice of the "Yeshu phenomenom." Not trained in Judaism at all <<and some rather looked askance of this Jewish backdrop>> ***their*** creation of "Yeshu" tended to be portrayed as, so to speak, "Jewish-Lite"; VERY Jewish lite. This "Jewish lite" orientation strayed from most of the caveats and traditions of the Jews. It was a generation or two posterior from the Crucifixion wherein this **NEW creation** of Yeshu {{and one which tended to "skip" the onerous *Halakha* without realizing that any "Yeshu" bereft of the Jewish *Halakha* was simply a "Yeshu" who never roamed our earth.}} took center place of what, in the final analysis, **be a GENTILE religion. AND NOT ONLY THAT; A GENTILE RELIGION WHICH LOOKED ASKANCE TOWARDS JUDAISM.*!!!!!!**

Think it through. Yes! Yeshu (Jesus) is hailed all over the place! Glory be to God. But the Yeshu of these Gentile Churches lacks the one thing which matters: A "Jesus" who lacks a genuine connection with his/her sheer 'JEWISHNESS' in the very marrow of one's bones. But of course the "Jesus"/Yeshu found in Christian Churches don't really understand that without "Jewishness" as the very heart of Yeshu's being there is no genuine Yeshu. Yes; of course: "Yeshu is Jewish." "Yeshu is Jewish" Yes. A hundred thousand Christian will swear that mantra: "Yeshu is Jewish." That's true, of course.

But then one finds out about the various multiple teachings of Christianity (((e.g., the Trinity))) which would decimate the very foundation of Judaism. I am speaking about the STRICT UNITY OF GOD which is the *sine non quo* without which there is no Judaism. In reality, that mantra "Yeshu is Jewish" is something of a façade. For that mantra is a convenience which allows Christians that they really love the Jewish Yeshu even though the rites and claims of Christianity are anathema to Judaism and anathama to the rites and beliefs of Judaism. If — somehow — Yeshu were to enter, say, a Roman Catholic Church service, just about everything would be radically anathema. Worst of all would be the claim of a TRIUNE GOD. The bed-rock of Judaism is the completely ONENESS of the God of the Jews.

Check at the very end of this manuscript. Christianity is Christianity and Judaism is Judaism. The two will never come together on this matter. Even so it is possible for both religions to join together with regard to what is called "Good Works."

*****   *****   *****   *****   *****
*****   *****   *****
*****   *****   *****   *****   *****

THIS "Yeshu," who never existed, gained great numbers of followers. Likewise, there were the self-ordained "Fathers of the Church" towards the end of the first century and onward. Christianity was not rooted in the true figure of "Yeshu"; the one and true one with "warts and all." These interlopers (especially the Fathers of the Church who held much power) created *out of thin air* a Yeshu with no warts at all. A figure who was perfect in all ways. In other words, not really a human being. There never were and never will be a perfect HUMAN being. To be Human is to be fallible. Hmmmmmmm. But somehow these "Fathers of the Church" came up — again with Hellenic tropes — A HUMAN WHO WAS PERFECT!!!!! A HUMAN WHO WAS GOD!!!!! **GLORY BE TO GOD!** A claim which is impossible. This was Yeshu's claim ((and it was Yeshu's claim back then)) which got the historical and true Yeshu crucified for this further blasphemy <see below>.

But pause for a moment. We have not — at least in this paragraph — brought up by the refrain by Yeshu himself. Herewith the blasphemy:

THE FATHER AND I ARE ONE

You will note that the "FATHERS OF THE CHURCH" were quick to advocate these strong words from Yeshu. By then — and largely set in motion because of this oxymoronic phrase was peddled by the Yeshu-figure day in and day out. After all, further — and well after the death of Yeshu — our quick Fathers of the Church created entrance by which a *TRI-partite* invention could be ratcheted up to what would be called as the famous "Holy **TRINITY**": "The Father"; "The Son" <i.e. Yeshu>; and something like a "Holy Spirit." It was referred to as "The Holy Trinity." Yeshu partly bears the onus for this insofar as he allowed for himself a duel-oriented blasphemy which would only become a greater Blasphemy.

*****

But closer to home in this production we shall concentrate on what Yeshu meant — when he said (and said often with the aura of command):

THE FATHER AND I ARE ONE

In any case Yeshu's refrain — and it has a somewhat vague aura with several possible meanings — can, at the least, appear to be a refrain by which Yeshu comforts himself here; and at other times eschews articulating the phrase aloud while he silently screams that HIS father (he came to know that Pantera was his father) should have taken more care to know his own child! All the other offspring from Miriam knew their fathers. Joseph spawned two or three offspring with Miriam before he died. Then Joseph's brother spawned — with Miriam — two or three further offspring. Yet Pantera, of course, made it his business to leave Miriam's shack in Nazareth way before either one of them would know if there was a conception. Three days and then he was gone and never came back. He had a wife and children. Chances are that the Sidonian Archer never saw Yeshu <albeit Yeshu combed the area of **SIDON**>.

Always, for Yeshu, was the pain of his missing father. All the other siblings had fathers who were with their baby offspring. But not for Yeshu; Pantera left Miriam not even knowing whether or not there had even been a conception.

*****   *****   *****

Now let us turn to the validity or invalidity of Yeshu's excoriations visited upon the Pharisees; was he being fair?

Again, and for the record, I do not recognize the validity of the Pharisaic invention of the putative Oral Torah. By and large, this whole production which you are reading <<that is, if there are ANY readers at all>> is predicated on the status of Scripture-centricity. But being Scripture-centric does not sanction that the *non-Scriptural* offerings of the PharisaicSect to the effect of the non-Scriptural mandates of the Pharisees are always self-aggrandizing. These forthcoming passages overstate the case against the Pharisees.}}

*****

YISHMAEL ben ABUYA

Matthew 15: 21—28.

From verse three onward to the end of the Chapter is pretty much a text largely orchestrated as an exercise in excoriating the Pharisees. Most of it is composed by the proto-Christian redactors who — two or three generations posterior to the actual situation given in the opening of the Chapter — are anxious to distinguish radically between Yeshu ((who at this time has been buried for a long time)) and the position of the Pharisees. The distance between Yeshu in the flesh and the position(s) of the Pharisees **then** is one thing. QUITE DIFFERNTLY is the time of this redaction <we are roughly talking soon after the first century ad> — is **HUGE** *compared to the distance between Yeshu and the Pharisees*.

The emergence of a proto-Christianity changed the landscape radically. The Pharisees were still fine. But the meaning of "Yeshu" had undergone **_radically_**. The reality is that the true Yeshu did not fit into the emergent contours In other words a new carved-out Yeshu which is now modeled to fit the requirements of the emergent Church. This Yeshu never lived at all; but it was what non-Jews wanted for this emergent "Church."

What about the Jews?

They lied low. They maintained their normal religion; the religion which maintained that there is but ONE — AND ONLY ONE — GOD. They <I> are here and, for the most part, doing well. We shall, of course, come back to these and other dimensions of this oldest religion with a Scripture.

There was and IS but ONE GOD. PERIOD! Yeshu's claim was, just by itself, blasphemous. By touting off that blasphemy —— **THE FATHER AND I ARE ONE** —— he radically put himself, in one sense, beyond the pale of Judaism, The strict UNITY of God is the bed-rock of Judaism. The blasphemy, again, also entailed the horrific implication that this *mamzer* was God.

What he said was way, way, terrible. Even so, there was about Yeshu — without anyone saying this — Yeshu is Jewish; now and forever. A Jew. A very faulty Jew. But Jew from birth to death. Yeshu was simply the kind of Jewishness which is carried in the very marrow of his bones. Don't get me wrong. He deserved what he got. HE BLAPHEMED. But for sure he was born Jewish (of a Jewish Mother); was circumcised; and lived as a Jew and died as a Jew. He was a Jew who ended up with a terrific black stain on tis life: flaunting his blasphemy. But this is to be noted as well: he helped many Jews who were having terrific hard times. Dare I say it? He did much good. His claim to Divinity was terrible. But Yeshu was Jewish to the marrow of his bones despite.

Yes. He — Yeshu — was a HUGE bothersome to the Pharisees and other groupings in Judaism. But on another level ((and he did this WITHOUT saying it)) there came over Yeshu towards the end of his life a deep remorse. Yeshu had now come to the genuine sadness which he visited to those close to him. ESPECIALLY, Miriam, the sister of Lazarus; she never successfully overcome the blow visited upon her. She honestly believed that Lazarus was dead and buried. It was cutting for her. But then to find out that the whole thing was a farce <albeit Yeshu did not want such an outcome> was too much for Miriam. She lost her appetite; radically. She died within three weeks of the sham Resurrection. **NOW** YESHU WANTED TO DIE. And he orchestrated his last days such that — he and ONLY he — would take the responsibility of what had happened at Bethany. He now wanted to die and he went through hell to do so.

*****

A note:

At some time, Yeshu had travelled to Egypt wherein he became astute with regard to potions and such paraphanalia. Some of the minor "miracles" were a function of the "magical" arts which he had consumed in Egypt. Some of the other 'miracles' were a function of his stature <he was taller than most Jews> combined with his overbearing personality. But the attempt of the "miracle of miracles" — the resurrection of Lazarus — fell flat on its face. Overwhelmingly, most Jews unmasked the fraud rather quickly.

This Egyptian sojourn by Yeshu had a number of significant reasons for the sojourn. One reason for the sojourn is gruesome. It appears that he chose to go to Egypt to have his testicles removed. Egyptian medical procedures were far more advanced with regard to surgery procedures. When he came back to Israel he let it be known that he had gone through the surgery. Yeshu indicated that such a procedure was a way to radically lesson any fornication; if at all. And the New Testament put forth that Yeshu made it clear that doing what HE did is NOT for all persons.

***** ***** *****

*****

***** ***** *****

But Saul/Paul was scheming to set in motion a **radically** reduced *Halakha, especially* with regard to dietary *Mitsvot* <and as well, the *halakhot* of the Pharisees>. He didn't fully understand the outcome of those puerile "Letters." But he, virtually, created Christianity. Saul was just a marginal Jew to begin with. His father was Jewish but his wife was not Jewish. And it is the woman — not the man — which carries Jewishness to the offspring.

Of course these Pauline developments came about after Yeshu died. I am certain that Yeshu (((that is if there is an after-life at all))) would have suffered much self-crimination to find out that this "Saul/Paul" ——— who never met Yeshu in the flesh ((albeit there were some, including "Saul/Paul" who claimed to have had an "apparition" of Yeshu which Saul/Paul and others who never met Yeshu in the alive flesh))) ——— **was rude enough to come and speak on behalf of Yeshu.** Basically it was a scam <<albeit those who had "apparitions" convinced themselves that such was real, and as well, those who claimed apparitions convinced themselves that this was real, and as well, those who had "apparitions" tended to find what they wanted from the putative "apparitions.">>

***** ***** *****

Never in a thousand years would Yeshu desire to have been the catalyst for what would become Christianity largely by the efforts of Saul/Paul who had never seen the flesh and blood of Yeshu. AND LO AND BEHOLD!!!! CHRISTIANITY. The emergence of Christianity was something which could have been cut off very quickly EXCEPT for one factor. I am referring to those puerile "Letters" of Saul/Paul wherein Saul/Paul painted a Yeshu who was made in the image and likeness of *SAUL/PAUL*. Yeshu <who was already dead> would have had little to offer to this emerging religion if he cared at all — and he didn't. Saul/Paul had an open field. He created a religion using the Pauline accounting of Yeshu <who was already dead> would have had little to offer this emerging religion if he even cared. And he didn't. The putative "Yeshu" of Christianity uses the NAME "Yeshu" but does not root Christianity in Judaism.

Christianity claims much about these things but eschews the fundamental JEWISHNESS which abides in Judaism. In other words, Christianity is NOT JUDAISM. AND THAT'S OK. What is NOT kosher is to claim Yeshu as the center piece of the Christian religion. In reality the putative "Yeshu" of Christianity — orchestrated by those "Fathers of the Church — is simply a so-called

"Yeshu" who never roamed on this Earth. It is a fabrication without flesh and blood. The true Yeshu, WARTS AND ALL, died as a Jew. Again, if Christianity insists on a perfect "Yeshu" they will be praying to an **IDOL**; that's the only true way of putting it. But that's up to those who follow Christianity.

*****

Yep: Indeed, Saul/Paul had an open field. He created a religion using the Pauline accounting of Yeshu>. Saul/Paul was on a "playground," so to speak, pronouncing this and that wherein this "this and that" and all-the-while had hardly anything real sense about Yeshu. But there was one thing which came out of his spiels useful for haters; these were the seeds of Christian Anti-Semitism. Congratulations.

*****   *****   *****   *****   *****

Yeshu and his Blasphemy.

THE FATHER AND I ARE ONE

This, of course, is the terrible blasphemy of Yeshu albeit Christianity would feed on that blasphemy and up-grade (so to speak) the whole matter to a putative "Trinity. The first blasphemy entails something like a "duo" <i.e. the blasphemy of Yeshu>; the second blasphemy is the one which is like a "trio" orchestrated in the second century by those swarmy "Fathers of the Church." In both cases —— this first one and then the second one —— violates the strict UNITY CHARACTRISTIC OF JUDAISM WHEN SPEAKING OF GOD. It is quite simple: **THERE IS BUT ONE GOD. PERIOD.** OUR Jewish God is neither a duality nor a trinity. Enough. Case closed.

Strict Unity in this matter is God. In the other two proposals the strict UNITY of Judaism is decimated, whether it is duality or a trinity. In the "smaller" case right before us we find that heading which was used by Yeshu* <a duality> falls limp in the face of the Pure UNITY WHICH IS GOD.

Accordingly, we will concentrate on which is put before with that claim of duality. I am speaking of Yeshu's phrasing above:

THE FATHER AND I ARE ONE

We shall return to this blasphemous model offered by Yeshu. But there are other tracks to be laid as we find out more about that curious man — the real one — "Yeshu."

*****   *****   *****

Father matters.

Yeshu being Yeshu would — possibly unconsciously — be drawn here to the area of **SIDON.** After all, his father was the **SIDONIAN** Archer. Yes, while there, Yeshu had helped a Cannanite woman to bring health to her daughter; and it worked. But that was not why he was there in the first place. Rather, it would seem, that Yeshu might just come across the **SIDON-ian Archer:** Pantera. But his hunt for the father gave no result. Listen:

Yeshu being Yeshu would — possibly unconsciously — be drawn again to ferret out the Sidonian Archer. But he never met his father. Yeshu being Yeshu, he could not just let it go.

The missing Father who left while all the other children from Miriam <the mother> had two stay-in (sequentially after the first died) genuine fathers. Of course there was before either of those two "regular" fathers <they were brothers> was Pantera who had bivouacked in Nazareth and who left three days after seeding Miriam and, as it turned out, he never came back to see if there was a conception. He left and put it behind him. He had his own family to deal with,

Yeshu twisted in his psyche about being a *mamzer*. He, Yeshu, actually went alone to visit his missing father. But when he got to the home of Pantera no-one was there and neighbors did not know where he was. The Roman Archer no longer lived there and his neighbors did not know whether or not he was dead. Perhaps he died; perhaps mortally wounded in a skirmish. Perhaps he moved. In any case Pantera could not be found. Who knows? More to the point it was Yeshu who took the absence to his heart; it still hurt even after all those years. Of course it was the missing Father which charged his brain even as an adult.

On the other hand there is a more serious matter. What Yeshu held as a comfort — his only comfort in that troubled man — turns out to be his blasphemous refrain:

THE FATHER AND I ARE ONE

However, the reality is that the short sentence is a blasphemy. The strict UNITY OF GOD is the most sacred bedrock of all Judaism. That phrase, then, it is anathema; it was Blasphemy.

97

YISHMAEL ben ABUYA

But in all that Yeshu did he — even when wayward — would and always identify as a Jew. A compromised Jew; but a Jew nonetheless. Yeshu — were he alive — would be the first to challenge *Saul/Paul*. Indeed he would cut-off Saul/Paul at the knees <so to speak> for casting — in those pathetic "letters"— "Yeshu" *in the image and likeness* of that scoundrel *SAUL/PAUL!*

We have also seen that Yeshu bandied about HIS blasphemy {for which he would pay the price} But when it comes to criminality Yeshu's fixation *vis a vis* that blasphemy pales in orders of magnitude compared to the ***deep criminality of Saul/Paul by — in effect — creating in those pathetic "letters" as a figure of himself and calling it "Yeshu."*** And there is something more. ***Saul/Paul was among disparate creators of Anti-Semitism*** (even if the heading had not yet emerged).

*****   *****   *****

And there was something else which wasn't "right" about Saul/Paul. HE WAS A ROMAN CITIZEN! in the very land of Israel WHICH WAS SUBJECTED TO HORRIBLE CONDITIONS **PRECISELY BY THE ROMAN OCCUPATION <u>OF JEWS IN THEIR OWN</u>**

NATION! <Again, cf. Eisenman> **WORSE** than that *Saul/Paul* had kept this feature under wraps, Now that *Saul/Paul* was undressed <in a manner of speaking> he — A ROMAN CITIZEN — would have no following. He disappeared and people forgot about him.

Fortunately —— albeit unfortunately would really be the reality ——Saul/Paul has been one of the factors involved in the creation of a Yeshu who — at heart **(as the story goes)** — was never really, really, Jewish at all. Within two generations after his death the figure of "Yeshu" was more and more presented <albeit not in theory> as a Gentile! Such seems ludicrous, of course. Yet such was pretty much the drift as those "Fathers of the Church" were creating a new religion.

*****

James/*Yaacob*, the second child of Miriam. He DID have the benefits of having a strong father. James and Yeshu got along even though they took vastly different "outcomes." James lived into the sixties. But not everything went well. In the Summer of the year 62 ce James was assassinated (by stoning) on and near the Temple Mount. The Roman weight had been thinned out that year

99

since more soldiers were needed for deployment for another uprising outside of Israel.

Early — soon after Yeshu was crucified — *Yaacob/* James would take the office of: "High Priest for the Poor and Disenfranchised" which, initially, had been planned for Yeshu. This was part of a diverse set of undertakings to draw off the steam of the onerous WEIGHT of the Roman Occupation. Yeshu — but then his brother, *Yaacob* — was put forth in that endeavor. Caiaphas and Pilate was trying to put forth a way of keeping the lower classes from Revolt which would be a MAJOR mistake. In other words a worthy distraction from schemes of Revolt which would only end in a total disaster.

*****   *****   *****

POST CRUCIFIXION.

James and Yeshu had gotten along even though they took vastly different "outcomes."

This was a time when <seventies ad> was the way of treating Yeshu, now that he was dead for some time. The net result of all this <<i.e., for those who were **inventing** an oxymoronic "Gentle Yeshu">> was to attempt to doctor these early documents, such as possible, from their true pedigree. They are scabs using the name of Yeshu without knowing at all what Yeshu was like.

*****

It is interesting that James/Yaacob, in the first place, actually came down from Nazareth and set up a kind of "retreat" <<about two months after Yeshu's Crucifixion>> for those who — despite his <Yeshu's>, of course> Blasphemy — wanted to honor what was good in Yeshu. James held on to the "retreat" for ten years and it was successful.

Curiously, that hopeless Roman, Saul/Paul, tried to be a member of the retreat. Saul/Paul was all about Saul/Paul and James wanted to get Saul/Paul out of the Community. Saul/Paul was only concerned with Saul/Paul and his pitiful "Letters": *exactly the kind of person who should NOT be in this Community.* To get Saul/Paul out of the Community James suggested that Saul/Paul go East to spread the "word" of Yeshu; and he did.

Unfortunately, Saul/Paul was good at creating a "Yeshu" made in the image and likeness of Saul/Paul. Even today the <u>Pauline</u> Yeshu fazes some people who they think they are honoring Yeshu

101

when, in fact, they are honoring Saul/Paul. After all there were hardly any dietary mandates. That, just by itself, shows how ignorant people can be. This "Pauline" factor is almost the antipathy of all that man who died on the cross.

MEDITATION EIGHT

Friday going into Saturday.

Unlike Yeshu, Jacob/James had Joseph as his father. Unlike some of his brothers and half-brothers, Jacob/James was never a disciple. He — Jacob — made his home in Nazareth until that weekend when Yeshu was put to death. {{{He, Jacob, was the one of three who came down surreptitiously <<but with the clearance of Caiaphas>> to bring the body back for a final burial in Nazareth. Yehuda and Shimon <but not the Shimon "The Rock"> were half-brothers who — in the dead of the night — removed Yeshu's corpse from a rich man who had allowed that Yeshu's remains could stay there until, roughly, when the corpse would be taken out and brought over to James' flat-bed on wheels (pulled by donkeys) which was would be used to get the coffin for transportation from Jerusalem and burial at Nazareth.}}}

*****

Later, by a bit over a two weeks of mourning, *Yaacob/James* would take the prepared office

103

of "High Priest (himself) for the Poor and Disfranchised" which, initially, had been planned for Yeshu. It was a great honor for James.

And there would be more. In addition James thought to set a retreat for many things but to mostly comment on what was good about Yeshu. With the Retreat led by James there would also siphoning off a growling population which was dying, little by little, by the heinous ROMAN OCCUPATION.

*****

Yeshu and Yakob had been very different in their respective avenues and psychic dispositions. But they loved and admired each other. Prior to that James was looking out for his slightly older brother who seemed never calm. Now Yeshu would have all the calm he could use.

*****

With the approval — already given — of Caiaphas ((who had cleared everything with Pilate in advance)) James took up the office which had been planned for Yeshu: "THE HIGH PRIEST OF AND FOR THE POOR AND DISENFRANCISED." This office included

— for the poor and disenfranchised — a time for the poor and the disenfranchised — a special time of honor whereby someone from the poor and disenfranchised would enter into the Holy of Holies in the Temple on YOM KIPPUR and, **ARTICULATING ALOUD THE TRUE NAME OF God!**

This honor — accorded to a non-Priest <and a Nazarene at that!> — was very much disputed by many Jews. But *Yaacob/James* prevailed since this "poor-man's" Office of High Priest effectuated the purpose of this James-led Community which was to siphon-off Revolutionary fervor among the poor and disenfranchised visited upon the cruel Occupation. For a number of years, this is how it went. But others with more "hef" brought back the "old way."

MEDITATION NINE

The true Yeshu did find some <u>substantial</u> fault with the invention of the putative Pharisaic Oral Torah since it was incorporated into the <Pharasaic> *Halakha* even though there was NO Scriptural foundation for doing such. But the Pharisees, lacking foundation for the endeavor, ignored foundations and just pushed ahead. That's how they got their way.

But never in a thousand years would the true Yeshu castigate openly the Pharisaic expanded dietary regimen (albeit, lacking Scriptural sanction). After all, the Pharisees had taken it upon themselves to do more in these matters. However, such was not really sanctioned and that also was wrong.

Yeshu in his heart maintained that the Oral Torah is NOT rooted in effect. The mandated standards found in Scripture are deeply rooted. In other words, the mandated *Mitsvot* are the gold standard. BUT THERE IS NO REAL SCRIPTURAL MANDATE **AT ALL** for the putative 'Oral Torah.'

That acknowledged, the Pharisees were fierce enemies of Yeshu since he harbored — and made a point of doing so — that blasphemy of which he would not let go. It was that horrible Blasphemy which he brought into his heart AND ALSO LET EVERYONE KNOW IT:

THE FATHER AND I ARE ONE

<<<SHAME ON YESHU>>>

***** ***** *****

The point is that Yeshu — when he was not In a mercurial melt-down — honored* the best received Groupings which largely constituted *BEIT YISRAL*. That's fine. But there was always the possibility of an explosion, ***ESPECIALLY SINCE HE CONTINUED TO HOLD ON TO A BLASPHEMY!***

> *. The "honoring" was both true and revealing. But there would have to be an asterisk in Yeshu's heart <so to speak> with regard to the Oral Torah SINCE THE VERY BEING OF THE ORAL

TORAH WAS BEREFT OF **ANY GROUNDING IN SCRIPTURE.**

***** ***** ***** ***** *****

***** ***** *****

***** ***** ***** ***** *****

One CAN imagine a "Paul" saying what he said in this forthcoming vicious diatribe <i.e., verses four through twenty-nine of *Matthew* 23. Also, one can easily imagine that the Christian redactors — about a century and a half after Yeshu died — created, basically, an anti-Jewish diatribe in the service of what would be called (with great presumption and grandiosity) "The New Testament." And, finally, I can easily see Yeshu himself <<albeit it is a different goal>> generating such tropes for Yeshu's actual <<<i.e., NOT the portrait given by the "Fathers of the Church">>> agendum. Yes, he was indeed, at times, mercurially 'over-the-top'.

If such words of mercuriality were from the mouth of Yeshu, it is Yeshu who thereby is demoted in stature. It is demeaning. But such mercurial outbursts were endemic for the flesh and blood of Yeshu. And I am sure that his half-brother, Jacob/James, would not allow Yeshu to speak that way. {{However, that's the problem. Jacob/

YISHMAEL ben ABUYA

James admired Yeshu and-yet pissed-off with his slightly older brother. But Jacob/James lived in Nazareth. Yeshu was seldomly there. THAT was the problem.}}

Whomever are the characters on both sides of this radically divisive diatribe, the over-all tone of this Meditation is to portray the Pharisees (along with the Scribes who disdained both the Pharisees and the mercurial Yeshu) in a bad light. Except for verses one through the first half of verse three of the Chapter, most of the Chapter is a reckless castigation of the Pharisees in particular and also of the Scribes. This would be expected given the agendum of the redactors <<<< i.e., the proto redactors would not want to acknowledge the reality that Yeshu was born Jewish; raised Jewish; and who died Jewish>>>>. Further, such conscious <so to speak> blindness on the part of the Christian redactors ((who didn't want the facts but who had decided in advance that there nothing 'really' Jewish in the make-up of Yeshu)) was both willful and pitiful. It was utterly ridiculous but that was THEIR faith. Had Yeshu lived impossibly long he would have nothing to do with such invented magic. Shame on the Christian redactors.

*****

110

Confusion is predictable when one is writing a story about Yeshu in such a way that Yeshu, so to speak, is not really Jewish. That self-refuting "story" is often sustained in certain portions of the Synoptics. Such, of course, is simply ludicrous just by itself; and it creates a text which is just as much ludicrous as the scene which inspires this text. Christians, when reading their rambling and mangled text, which is the New Testament, **should** feel embarrassed by virtue of the constant agendum of the Christian redactors who formed The New Testament such that, even now, pretend that Yeshu was not "really" a Jew. {{{And for that matter recall this: his mother was a Jew; all the Apostles were Jews; Joseph was a Jew. They all died as Jews.}}}

There is a curious wrinkle in this whole accounting of Yeshu. HIS <Yeshu's> Blasphemy <<and we will have much to say about his Blasphemy>> was a pointer to what the Christian religion made of a **triad**, if you will, a trinity if you will; composed of **THREE!!! Gods. God The FATHER; God The SON; God The HOLY GHOST; or God THE HOLY SPIRIT.** One; Two; Three GODS some would say; in other words — according to some — a Blasphemy. But keep in mind it was the Blasphemy put forth by Yeshu who opened up the idea that — somehow — "GOD" is two. So why not three? Why not forty-three Gods?

The adherents will cry out "FAITH."

If "faith" is understood as **fides**/fidelity I am all for it. If "faith" is taken as the Hebrew "**EMUNAH**" <TRUST> I am all for it.

What is to be eschewed, however, is to cry out for just about anything and call it "FAITH." "Faith" or no "Faith" GOD IS GOD AND A HUMAN IS A HUMAN. They are not the same. GOD IS PERFECT; NO HUMAN IS PERFECT. To pretend that GOD CAN BE HUMAN AND GOD AT THE SAME TIME is just ridiculous. VICE VERSA such is just that: pretend. It certainly is not "FAITH."

*****

"Trust" is not sufficient for "Emunah." Dig in to it. You will be rewarded.

***** ***** ***** ***** *****
***** ***** *****
***** ***** ***** ***** *****

MEDITATION TEN

Expanding now to all four Gospels. The emerging Christian religion desperately wanted *ITS* YESHU. In so doing the emerging Christian religion [and on up into the twenty-first century] ended up with a Yeshu **who simply never existed**. Again; let it sink in. This impossible dream created a Yeshu who simply never existed; just a dream. Such was the great anxiety in the first two centuries of the Common Era as the Christians attempted to square the circle.

The major figure is Yeshu ((short for Yehoshua; i.e., Yeshu///Joshua; Josh)). Yeshu was born a Jew*; was circumcised; was raised as a Jew; and was an idiosyncratic preacher/instigator who felt he had an essential message to bring *Beit Yisrael* <<a message, as we shall see, which was a blasphemy>>. And Yeshu died a Jew. {{There is more information on this blasphemy in several parts of this book.}}

> *. Of course the first born <male or female> receives Jewishness from the mother; and, indeed, all the Jewish

113

infants receive their Jewishness from the mother.

In any case, Yeshu was — even as an adult — special in the eyes of his doting mother even though HE was embarrassed that his mother's first child was a *mamzer*. There would be two more offspring from Miriam by way of Joseph, and then — after Joseph died — two or more offspring from Mariam by way of Joseph's brother.

*****

It was *Jacob*/James <the first of Miriam's offspring by Joseph> who was closest in birth to Yeshu *the mamzer*. In any case, Yeshu was the progeny by way of Miriam the archer Pantera, an archer <he was Jewish>, conscripted into the Roman Army who bivouacked in Miriam's house (more like a roomy shed) in Nazareth.

Yeshu's mother, keep in mind, was a "Hairdresser" <<i.e., a "Magdala", a maiden with loose morals.>>

As we have seen, Miriam's subsequent offspring had valid wives or husbands. Yeshu alone, was her offspring by way of a man who was not "Kosher." Yeshu, you will see, even in the New Testament, was somewhat shamed by virtue of the Hairdresser whose first offspring was a *mamzer*. Indeed, the New Testament allows Yeshu to be put forth as "edgy" with regard to his mother by virtue of the Pantera factor.

*****

The to be cited passages will testify, Yeshu's self-appointed "mission" was one which explicitly ***eschewed any overtures to the Gentiles***.*

> *. The one exception was the accounting of the Cannanite woman who pestered Yeshu to do something for her sick daughter (who was not with her). Her insistent pestering was more than he, Yeshu, could take. He agreed to do what it would take for the daughter to survive (and did). But not before he rattled the mother with two caveats which made it clear that his mission **was NOT geared to non-Jews.** Listen again: LET IT SINK IN!
>
> **I WAS SENT <u>ONLY</u> FOR THE LOST SHEEP OF YISRAEL**
>
> and

YISHMAEL ben ABUYA

IT IS NOT JUST TO TAKE THE CHILDREN'S FOOD AND TOSS IT TO THE HOUSE DOGS

Just **WHEN** will Christians wake-up to the fact that the "Jesus" of Christianity never walked on this Earth. The two statements above make it clear for everyone who honor TRUTH.

ENCORE: Some know this already. Others struggle to make a circle a square. Others just float down the river and pray to a figure who never walked on this Earth. Repetition can be Godly. This is certainly Godly. You must bring these words from Yeshu and let it sink in.

SO AGAIN BRING OUT THESE TWO CAVEATS. If you understand this you will understand that Yeshu is LARGELY **NOT** concerned with non-Jews. To wit:

I WAS SENT <u>ONLY</u> FOR THE LOST SHEEP OF ISRAEL

IT IS NOT JUST TO TAKE THE CHILDREN'S FOOD AND TOSS IT TO THE HOUSE DOGS

TRUE AND STRONG CAVEATS. The first caveat says it all. What I write now — just the first line — so as to sting the gentiles and, more importantly, to wake up JEWS to their patrimony.

ENCORE THEN AND TAKE IT TO HEART!:

I WAS SENT <u>ONLY</u> FOR THE LOST SHEEP OF ISRAEL

*****

Continuing on.

His mother, keep in mind, was a "Hairdresser" <i.e., a "Magdala," a maiden with loose morals>>.* As we have seen, Miriam's subsequent offspring had valid wives or husbands. Yeshu alone, was her offspring by of the man who was — so to speak — not "kosher." Yeshu, you will see, even in the New Testament, Yeshu was shamed by the "Hairdresser" whose first offspring was a *mamzer*. Indeed, the New Testament actually allowed Yeshu to be put forth as "edgy" with regard to Miriam; the "Magdala"-the "hairdresser." (In other words, two names for the same person.) Then a "Magdelina" is put into the equation as to puzzle the situation.

Miriam is Mariam. Because of her reputation she was also referred to as a "Hair-dresser" <i.e. "Magdala." Two names for one person>>. So far, so good. But the New Testament supplied "Magdalena" who was only a name so as to confuse the situation. But on the Thursday night before Good Friday a true "Magdalena" arrives and insists on washing Yeshu's feet. Miriam (i.e., the mother of Yeshu) poses as a "Magdelina." Yeshu lets his mother wash his feet for the last time. There was absolute quiet tears all around.

There would still be horrors before the night was over; the dreadful Roman whipping. But even that seemed not to have brought a big change in Yeshu. It was time to face the horror of Thursday night and virtually the whole of Friday. He was on a plane which most humans never imagine.

MEDITATION ELEVEN

ENCORE:

It is clear that the Gospels in some places are high-jacked by subsequent redactors who lusted for a Yeshu who is not Jewish: a Yeshu who is NOT Jewish to the marrow of one's bones. But such is ludicrous. And THAT is precisely why the New Testament is constantly acting in bad-faith. For *those* authors create a "Yeshu" which is but a façade. ***AGAIN: A YESHU WHO IS NOT JEWISH TO THE BONE MARROW IS SMPLY <u>NOT</u> YESHU*** (warts and all)

***** ***** *****

Of course these Pauline developments came after Yeshu died. I am certain that Yeshu (((that is, if there is an after-life at all))) would have suffered much recrimination were he, Saul/Paul, had anything at all with the early launching of what would call itself "Christianity." His "Letters" gave so many people to eschew Judaism and, further, gave Judaism a bad and false accounting. Never in a thousand years would Yeshu desire to have been the catalyst for what would become — Christianity — most of which is from Saul.

Notification:

<<<And here is pause for acknowledging the figure of Yeshu in a bad way. His concentration on his Blasphemy was damning for Judaism. Just for the record.>>>

*****

But in all that Yeshu did he — even when wayward — would always identify as a Jew and NOT anything else but a Jew. Of course Yeshu was dead by the time Saul/Paul came into the equation. Indeed Yeshu — had he was still alive (which he wasn't) — would have cut-off at the knees of Saul/Paul for casting "Yeshu" *in the image and likeness* of that scoundrel Saul/Paul.

Turning to Yeshu. We have seen that Yeshu bandied about Yeshu's fixation for his blasphemy. And he paid the price for such. But when it comes to **criminality Yeshu's fixation on that Blasphemy <<i.e., THE FATHER AND I ARE ONE>>** {for which he suffered a terrible retribution} pales in orders of magnitude compared to the **deep criminality of Saul/Paul**

120

by — in effect — creating a figure of himself and calling it "Yeshu" knowing that Yeshu was dead and could not abort this Pauline criminality.

Saul/Paul was one of the creators of Anti-Semitism. And if the phrase "Anti-Semitism" was not yet "coined" at this stage, the REALITY of Anti-Semitism was on the march.

*****

———— But Saul/Paul {{who never saw Yeshu in the flesh}} was already scheming to set in motion a radically reduced *Halakha*, especially with regard to the dietary *Mitsvot* <and as well the *halakhot* of the Pharisees>. Saul/Paul didn't fully understand the outcome. But he virtually set in motion the early parameters of Christianity. Again, Saul/Paul didn't fully understand the outcome; but he virtually created Christianity.

The founding father of what would be called "Christianity" was Saul/Paul; **NOT YESHU**. Had Yeshu been alive at that time he would have made sure that this interloper would have NO STANDING **AT ALL**. From this time on most of the usage "Yeshu" (or, later, "Jesus" for English) became, in effect, a fraud and largely remains so to this day. It's wild when one thinks about this. The central reality is that Yeshu/Jesus would never understand the emergent Church even though these "proto Jesuits" <so to say> created out of thin air with *their* creation of Yeshu which was sliced AWAY from the true **JEWISH REALITY OF THE LIVING YESHU**. Since Yeshu was now dead these "proto Jesuits" had the open field to CREATE the Yeshu which they wanted for their blossoming religion.

It is pitiful. The central figure died remained in his grave. From this time forward and into the twenty-first century there were many visions of "Yeshu" but virtually all those visions were largely NOT the reality of the **JEWISH** "Yeshu." A claim of "Yeshu" which is not rooted in Judaism is simply an unconscious scam.

In any case know that the famous "Yeshu" was raised as a Jew and had no other religious identity. Period.

Yes but no. There was that serious fixation on the part of Yeshu with his Blasphemy. That is sad and it is a stain on his Jewishness. It was wrong: This "Father"— oriented Blasphemy. That is sad and it is a stain on his Jewishness. ((Indeed it was his tie to this Blasphemy <which he would not let

go> which got Yeshu into trouble; big trouble.)) It was wrong. The "FATHER and I are ONE." This Blasphemy was a foolish rooted claim which is not compatible with Jewish accountings of there being just **ONE GOD; <u>PERIOD</u>**.

*****   *****   *****

But in all that Yeshu did, he — even when he was wayward — would always identify as a Jew and NOT anything else than but a Jew. If you hear the name "Yeshu" <aka: "Jesus"> know that the famous 'Jesus' was raised as a Jew and had no other religious identity. Period.

Yes. There was that serious fixation on the part of Yeshu with regard to his Blasphemy. That is sad and it is a stain on his Jewishness. It was wrong. The "Father"-oriented Blasphemy hangs heavy. <u>Indeed</u> it is sad and it is a stain on his Jewishness. It was wrong. This "Father"-oriented Blasphemy was a foolish claim which is not compatible with Jewish accountings of there being ONE GOD **PERIOD. Yes!** Don't *"pooh pooh"* the Blasphemous claim; again, it is a serious stain on his Jewishness with regarding accountings of there being just ONE GOD **PERIOD**. Yes! All of that. Even so, this man, Yeshu, — in my book — the sacred *mantra* <longer version> prevails in this case. He was born a Jew by way of a Jewish mother; he was circumcised; participated in all the Holy Days as a child and as an adolescent (and, I presume, he did so as a grown man); and rarely did he interchange with non-Jews <except for monetary exchanges>.

And there is this. It goes against Jewish law. There were credible indications by Yeshu himself. There were some rumors — but credible rumors — that Yeshu went to Egypt to have his testicles removed so as not to be able to have intercourse. Who knows? He did, eventually, indicate that the rumor was correct AND even explained to others why he underwent that procedure: It is difficult to have intercourse is one's testicles are gone. To his credit he acknowledged that such should not be such doing for most people. After all, it is difficult to have intercourse without testicles. Doing such is only for a few, he maintained. Without intercourse, most of the population would not (could not?) go in that direction. If only for a few. After all, {{{at least before modern science which takes care of many things}}} without intercourse the species would die out and that would be wrong.

But Yeshu's primary target was himself. He lusted and he eschewed such for "The Kingdom."

But there really IS something about Yeshu which <u>requires </u>not only further examination, but something which should be attended to SOON. I am speaking about Yeshu's fixation on his famous blasphemy.

THE FATHER AND I ARE ONE

This is the easy level. It is easily adjudicated. The phrase just hangs there and no-one notices.

The hard one is this: The phrase turns out to be a Blasphemy which, in effect, challenges the very root of Judaism where-in the matter and the corollary thereof is to be disputed. Because the corollary is religious in a certain way such that it which will jumble some heavy feathers. We are concerned with such a BLASPHEMY. I am speaking of the phrase above which was dear to Yeshu with fierce significance.

*****

However there was a more complex matter on the side of Judaism. Yeshu was a Jew. Period. He was a Jew who blasphemed. Period. What do you with such a man? It's relatively easy. Any way you look at it you will find that Yeshu apostatized by virtue by his Blasphemy; he was out of the fold; technically. But a "technicality" is just that. His apostatization didn't take away his very solid roots in Judaism: a Jew rooted in the very marrow of his bones. It will always be the case that this Jew — apostatized or not — never stopped being JEWISH. Period.

On the other hand the emergence of Christianity created a ridiculously "Yeshu"/Jesus which never existed. For me, I would allow two things. The true Yeshu is dead and buried in Nazareth. Yeshu is dead and buried <in Nazareth>; that's just reality. The other fold entails the fact that the putative "Yeshu" created out of nothing by those "Fathers of the Church" was just a kind of façade. Something which for a "nice and proper" image for Sunday mass. However, in any case our **JEWISH** blasphemer was real. As for me, give the blasphemer <with good intent> over a nothing which never roamed on this Earth.

Put it this way: He is dead and buried. Blasphemer or not (and he did blaspheme) he was Jewish AND — **unlike the putative "Yeshu"/Jesus created out of nothing by those "Fathers of the Church** — OUR Jewish blasphemer was real. Again, as for me, give me the blasphemer <with

good intent> over a "wishy/washy" nothing who never roamed this Earth.

***** ***** ***** ***** *****
***** ***** *****
***** ***** ***** ***** *****

And there was something else which wasn't "right" about Saul/Paul. HE WAS A ROMAN CITIZEN! in the very land of Israel WHICH WAS SUBJECTED TO HORRIBLE CONDITIONS **PRECISELY BY THE ROMAN OCCUPATION <u>FOR JEWS IN THE OWN NATION!</u>** <Again, cf. Eisenman.> Worse than that, Saul/Paul kept this feature under wraps FOR YEARS! Only when Saul/Paul was in desperate straits by virtue of his own actions did this prevaricator play his Roman card to save his sorry life.

Saul/Paul was one of the factors involved in the creation of a Yeshu who — at heart (**as the story goes**) — was never really, really Jewish at all. Within two generations the figure of "Yeshu" (who, of course, was already dead) was more and more presented <albeit not in theory> as a Gentile. Such is ludicrous, of course. But that was pretty much the drift, especially after Jacob/James was assassinated (by stoning) in the Summer of

62 ad on and near the Temple Mount. The culprit had to eliminate Jacob/James who had documents which some wanted certain documents so as to skew them in such a way that Yeshu would be something of a 'Pansy.' The net result of all of this <<i.e., for those who were inventing an oxymoronic "Gentile Yeshu>> who was now fabricated.

*****

IT IS A DISGRACE THAT THE SO-CALLED "Letters" OF SAUL/PAUL ARE BROUGHT INTO ANY SANCTURARY.

*****

There was and IS but ONE GOD; PERIOD!

Yeshu's claim was, just by itself, blasphemous. By touting off the blasphemy: *THE FATHER AND I ARE ONE* he radically put himself beyond the pale of Judaism <in one sense>. The strict UNITY OF GOD is the bed-rock of Judaism. Further, the blasphemy (in this case) also entailed the horrific implication that this *mamzer* was God!

*****   *****   *****

The reality is that Yeshu had proclivities which were seeded in his psyche when he found, in the course of his life, his status as a *mamzer*. He was never settled in his own skin; he wanted, desperately, to stand-out of the ordinary. He DID indeed stand-out as he —— a human like you or me except he sought no normal adulation but, rather, 'over-the-top' adulation —— was not settled in his own psyche. He always wanted to be on a stage. Towards the end —— but before the scam Resurrection of Lazarus —— he managed to get significant adulation from a fair amount of Jews. But such was not enough for his hungry soul. This drive for adulation led him to arranging A HYPER MIRACLE <in his mind> *SO AMAZING THAT IT WOULD EVEN CAUSE THE PHARISEES TO UNDERSTAND, FINALLY, THAT* "THE FATHER AND I ARE ONE." But, as it turned out, that forthcoming hyper — <but putative> — Miracle only made the Pharisees, first, and sometime later, others, just how **TAWDRY** the whole thing was. **AND WORSE FOR YESHU,** just how BLASPHEMIC he came across to more and more Jews as he CONTINUED loud and clear that **HUGE BLASPHEMY**:

YISHMAEL ben ABUYA

___THE FATHER AND I ARE ONE___

*****   *****   *****

Yes. Yeshu was a HUGE bothersome to the Pharisees and other groupings in Judaism. But on another level ((and he did this WITHOUT saying it)) there came over a deep remorse visited upon Yeshu. Yeshu had now come to understand the genuine sadness which he had now visited upon those who were affected by his own stupidity by virtue of **his** gigantic stupidity. Most of all, he dwelled deep into his heart knowing that now Miriam <the sister of Lazarus> had been **radically** affected and it seemed like she would die. {{And she did within a month.}} He wanted to die. And to his credit he did what it would take to do so.

*****

This "Resurrection Miracle" occurred just five days before the "Great Shabbat" (and called the "Great Shabbat" by virtue of the fact that it was also the first day of *Pesakh*). The original intent ((sent in motion by Caiaphas with the "sign-off" of Pilate)) was to radically "upgrade" the status of this controversial figure <"Yeshu">. The idea was that Yeshu would be appointed as the High

Priest for the poor and disenfranchised. Yeshu was, then, actually appointed as the High Priest of and for the poor and disenfranchised. The hope was to siphon-off some of the growing balloon <so to speak> of revolutionary activity which might spark into a Revolt against the Roman Occupation. Caiaphas understood that a Revolt against Rome would be a disaster; indeed the Temple just might be destroyed.

*****

Caiaphas, of course, understood the situation. But soon after his appointment Yeshu started to act strangely. Caiaphas had already sensed an erratic vein in Yeshu's comportment, especially after taking his role. Caiaphas couldn't really depend on Yeshu, even though he was liked by the Poor and Disenfranchised. Caiaphas had to make a change in "The Plan." Yeshu was too erratic as it turned out. Caiaphas decided that there would be a change in "The Plan." Yeshu's brother, Jacob, came down from Nazareth and Caiaphas decided that there would be a substantial change in "The Plan." To be sure, Yeshu must have been embarrassed with the change whereby James — not Yeshu — who would now be the one who would take on the mantle of the High Priest for the Poor and Disenfranchiesd. Yeshu was quiet on these matters; but it hurt.

*****

There is a spectrum for the meaning of a "Jewish Messiah." Most claims of being a Messiah back then had the connotation of a military figure. And Pilate most certainly focused on a military figure. But there were also messianic claims which did not necessarily require a military figure. Yeshu, of course, was not a military figure. So the back and forth between the two figures rendered a stalemate. Pilate got tired of this debate with Yeshu. Pilate decided to subject this curious figure who was so strange to be subjected to a Roman whipping ((the worst and the bloodiest)). Pilate then sent Yeshu back to Caiaphas with the understanding that Caiaphas could decide to do whatever with the prisoner. Further, IF Caiaphas decided to find Yeshu as guilty, the punishment would be Crucifixion. Caiaphas got what he wanted.

*****   *****   *****

Early on that early evening ((before Yeshu was reprimanded to Pilate)) it was clear that Yeshu was saying things which made some of his followers to say that Yeshu wanted to die. Shimon <but not the Shimon known as "The Rock"> and Judas were in charge of the group's treasury. They were especially concerned with Yeshu. He indeed seemed to want to die. They were both concerned and left early even before the matter of the blasphemy came up. It was common knowledge that Yeshu was very close to his brother, Jacob, in Nazareth. The two of them, Shimon and Judas* used the money to get donkeys so they could get to Nazareth quickly as possible so as to get his brother, Jacob, could get to Nazareth as quickly as possible so as to get his favorite brother, Jacob, get down to Jerusalem on time.

> *. {{Judas got a bum deal in many accounts. The simple truth was that Judas was but the treasurer of the on again off again "apostles" who were the followers of Yeshu. Period.}}

Later that Thursday night most of the "apostles" laid low since so many of them were afraid since it became known that somehow Yeshu was in chains. This was more than most of the "apostles" could bear when finding out that Yeshu was dressed in chains. Rumors were all over and mostly false. In any case, Yeshu was dressed in chains for a rump-*SANHEDRIN* in the huge dining room of

Caiaphas who was trying to mitigate the whole affair. Caiaphas gave several times to persuade Yeshu to drop his blasphemy. But Yeshu was hell-bent to maintain his treasured blasphemy <even though it would kill him>.

Getting back to Judas. The money ((which was not that much at all)) was allocated to send two Apostles that night on donkeys so as to get to Jacob's home in Nazareth and to quickly return to Jerusalem *pronto*.

They got there about two hours after midnight. Jacob was not surprised. He knew Yeshu inside/out. Jacob had a flat-bed vehicle. He arranged it that the donkeys would pull the flat-bed vehicle. He arranged it that the donkeys would pull the flat-bed vehicle with the three: Judas; Shimon <"the Rock"> and Jacob back to Jerusalem.

They arrived in Jerusalem in early morning and went to the home of Caiaphas. He insisted to come into his homestead. Yes. Yeshu was under arrest and would be Crucified. He suggested that all three of them stay at his home; watching a Crucifixion is not something

one would embrace. Besides, there were things to take care of.

*****

Yes. He had been a HUGE bothersome to the Pharisees and other groupings in Judaism. But on another level (and he did this WITHOUT saying this) there came over Yeshu a deep remorse in those last five days. In particular, Yeshu had now come to the deep genuine sadness which he had visited upon those close to him ((Miriam, the sister of Lazarus, especially)). He wanted to die. And to his credit, he did what it would take to do so.))

*****   *****   *****

{The Pharisees, as we have seen, dietary mandates are huge matters whereas the Scriptural dietary mandates are of very significant weight, yet they do not come close the energy involved with regard to dietary mandates. Keep this in mind.}

*****

It is clear that the Gospels in some places are high-jacked by subsequent redactors of the New Testament who would just LUST for a Yeshu who is not Jewish; in other words, a Yeshu who is NOT Jewish to his bones, and better, just "Jewish lite." Such is simply ludicrous; indeed it is impossible: A Jew is a Jew whether she/he is observant or not. And THAT is precisely why the New Testament is constantly acting in bad faith. For those authors created a "Yeshu" which is a façade. Again. YES AGAIN: *A YESHU WHO IS NOT TIED TO THE BONE MARROW OF HIS BEING IS SIMPLY NOT YESHU* {warts and all}.

But there is one condemnation of the Pharisaic position by Yeshu which condemnation is perfectly congruent with Yeshu's Scripture-centric approach to the HALAKHA. But even then, when and as Yeshu puts forth that the *MITSVOT* of Scripture and ONLY the *MITSVOT* of Scripture constitutes proper observance he is met, of course, with a condescending critique by the Pharisees — if he's lucky. Chances are that the Pharisaic leaders would scourge Yeshu for limiting the true *Halakha* in these matters.

Yeshu does not excoriate, then, in this particular situation, even as he disagrees with them. ((((However, it is to be noted, disagreement **does** become excoriation of the Pharisees, it appears, with the New Testament's redactor's accounting of Yeshu's refutation of the Pharisaic position in Chapter Twenty-Three as *per* the New Testament.))) In any case, Yeshu calmly dismisses the Pharisaic claim insofar as their claims go beyond the mandate of Scripture and wherein such "going beyond" of the Scriptural mandates constitutes, just by itself, **a violation** of a famous Scriptural mandate. God is on Yeshu's side. Listen, and take it to heart. Listen:

ALL THAT I MANDATE TO YOU, YOU MUST KEEP AND OBSERVE, <u>ADDING NOTHING TO IT, AND TAKING NOTHING AWAY</u>.

[*Deuteronomy 13:1*]

*****

Accordingly, he, Yeshu, castigates these other "inventions" of the Pharisees. Here is his voice is, initially, more condescending than vitriolic. Yes. As we shall see below, both Yeshu and the Pharisees are quite capable of spuming vitriol upon each other. Herewith is how Yeshu chooses to castigate the Pharisees without villainizing them:

ENCORE

YISHMAEL ben ABUYA

Any plant my Father has not planted will be pulled up by the roots. Leave them [the Pharisees] . They are blind leading men leading blind men. [15:14]

__Jewish readers of Yeshu will have the full confidence that this__

HUMAN MAN AND ONLY HUMAN MAN *IS NO GOD AT ALL.*

BUT OF COURSE!

Yeshu was but a human. Yes. He *__claimed, in effect, in effect, to be God__* <albeit in a curious way>

Indeed his blasphemy ((which he displayed often)) says as much:

"THE FATHER AND I ARE ONE"

Anybody can claim just about anything. BUT <u>CLAIMING SUCH </u>does not constitute reality.

In any case, as the Yeshu to be cited will testify, his self-appointed "mission" was one which explicitly ***eschewed any overtures to the Gentiles***.

****

AN AUTHOR'S NOTE

Throughout the whole manuscript I have treated the Christianity as a kind of false religion insofar that the "Yeshu" of Christianity is <u>not at all</u> the "Yeshu" <i.e., the real and living "Yeshu/"Jesus"> for Judaism by a long shot. So much could be said on this matter but I eschew to do such here. Rather than making my case about the falseness of the "Yeshu" in Christianity I would rather, at this time, to celebrate something wondrous **IN OUR TIME** on the part of Christians.

The dedication of this book brings to mind the horror of **THE SIX MILLION** which obtained, roughly the time of that pitiful man ((but he was no man)), who orchestrated an infamous hell, for mainly Jews, which came to be during his hellish reign. The words for this horror cannot be found. So I will stop here.

LO and BEHOLD! Christianity across the spectrum did NOT pretend that the above was not THEIR business. Virtually ALL the varieties of Christianity poured out their money and heart-felt support. t

141

Christianity is Christianity and Judaism is Judaism. We can work together.

My Prayer:

Thank-You, God, for being alive

Thank-You for all the good things in my life

Please help me to understand to the best of my limits and to <u>know</u> that I belong to You, <u>H</u>ashem

And that You, <u>H</u>ashem, are always there on the other side of my fear

Post Script

Meghan Kathleen Stahl

Whatever her circumstances may be — even in darkest hell — she brings in the sunlight.

Printed in the United States
By Bookmasters